T0323613

Cambridge Elements ≡

Elements in the Problems of God
edited by
Michael L. Peterson
Asbury Theological Seminary

RELIGIOUS TRAUMA

Michelle Panchuk
Murray State University

CAMBRIDGE
UNIVERSITY PRESS

CAMBRIDGE
UNIVERSITY PRESS

Shaftesbury Road, Cambridge CB2 8EA, United Kingdom

One Liberty Plaza, 20th Floor, New York, NY 10006, USA

477 Williamstown Road, Port Melbourne, VIC 3207, Australia

314–321, 3rd Floor, Plot 3, Splendor Forum, Jasola District Centre,
New Delhi – 110025, India

103 Penang Road, #05–06/07, Visioncrest Commercial, Singapore 238467

Cambridge University Press is part of Cambridge University Press & Assessment,
a department of the University of Cambridge.

We share the University's mission to contribute to society through the pursuit of
education, learning and research at the highest international levels of excellence.

www.cambridge.org
Information on this title: www.cambridge.org/9781009539012

DOI: 10.1017/9781009269643

First published 2024

A catalogue record for this publication is available from the British Library.

ISBN 978-1-009-53901-2 Hardback
ISBN 978-1-009-26967-4 Paperback
ISSN 2754-8724 (online)
ISSN 2754-8716 (print)

Religious Trauma

Elements in the Problems of God

DOI: 10.1017/9781009269643
First published online: December 2024

Michelle Panchuk
Murray State University

Author for correspondence: Michelle Panchuk, mpanchuk@murraystate.edu

Abstract: When religion is the site of abuse and trauma, it can deeply impact a person's ability to relate to God and engage in spiritual practice. As such, religious trauma is ripe for philosophical exploration. Section 1 of this Element provides a brief history of the concept of psychological trauma, contemporary accounts of its neurobiological basis, and its impact on human agency. Section 2 sketches a model of religious trauma through the first-person narratives of survivors and emerging psychological data. Section 3 explores the social epistemology of religious trauma, focusing on how failures of knowledge create space for religious abuse and the insights of survivors may help communities guard against it. The last two sections consider three perennial topics in philosophy of religion from the perspective of religious trauma: the problem of evil, the problem of divine hiddenness, and religious experience.

This Element also has a video abstract: www.cambridge.org/EPOG-Panchuk

Keywords: religious trauma, problem of evil, spiritual abuse, religious experience, religious epistemology

ISBNs: 9781009539012 (HB), 9781009269674 (PB), 9781009269643 (OC)
ISSNs: 2754-8724 (online), 2754-8716 (print)

Contents

Prologue

A few decades ago, the term "religious trauma" would have conjured images of obscure, but sensational, accounts of religious cults. But as I write this Element, awareness of the physical, psychological, and spiritual harm that can be inflicted even in mainstream religious contexts has reached an all-time high. This month two documentaries aired, revealing systematic abuses and their cover up in different pockets of evangelicalism ("Hillsong: A Megachurch Exposed" and "Shiny Happy People: Duggar Family Secrets"); an attorney general recently determined that 451 Catholic clergy abused over 2,000 children since 1950 in the Diocese of Illinois ("Hundreds of Catholic Clergy in Illinois Sexually Abused Thousands of Children, AG Finds" 2023); and just last year an internal investigation revealed the cover-up of over 700 abusive pastors and lay-leaders in the Southern Baptist Convention (Guidepost Solutions 2022). On Netflix one can choose from documentaries about abuse in Mormonism, Scientology, Hasidic Judaism, by hot yoga founder Bikram Choudhury, and even one on how to become a cult leader! And a quick internet search reveals several articles written in the past three years about spiritual abuse in Muslim contexts (Issa 2021; Waley et al. 2022).

Even as the general public is horrified and entertained by such accounts, deep understanding of the unique contours of trauma inflicted in religious contexts remains elusive, not only in popular culture, but also within religious communities themselves and among psychologists and clinical professionals. Therapists learn to address the trauma of physical, sexual, and emotional abuse, but often remain unequipped to grasp their spiritual significance when tied to religion. Religious communities encourage survivors to amend beliefs and practices to achieve "healthier" or "more accurate" religious lives and theologies, but fail to comprehend the underlying neurobiological reality of trauma or their own culpability for creating the conditions for abuse. Alicia Crosby notes that while religious trauma may be one of the most pervasive forms of trauma in the world, it is systematically "invisibilized" by religious institutions and the broader culture and remains shrouded in silence (Crosby 2020: 20). This Element is neither a guide for clinical professionals nor a handbook for religious leaders. It employs the tools of analytic philosophy of religion to elucidate the phenomenon of religious trauma, demonstrating that the physical, psychological, and spiritual impact are often inseparable in the lived experience of survivors. However, in so doing, it may offer insight not only to philosophers of religion, but to all who wish to understand and ameliorate the harm.

The Element proceeds as follows. The first section provides a brief history of the concept of psychological trauma, contemporary accounts of its neurobiological basis, and its impact on human agency. The second sketches a model of religious trauma through the first-person narratives of survivors and emerging psychological data. Section 3 explores the social epistemology of religious trauma, focusing on how failures of knowledge create space for religious abuse and the insights of survivors may help communities guard against it. The last two sections consider three perennial topics in philosophy of religion from the perspective of religious trauma: the problem of evil, the problem of divine hiddenness, and religious experience.

While religious trauma can happen in any religious community, because this Element is part of the "Problems of God" series, I limit my analysis to religious trauma in monotheism, specifically Judaism, Christianity, and Islam. The account may be generalizable to other religious contexts in some helpful ways, but it may not be applicable in others. I hope scholars take up such research in the future. The work is also limited by my own positionality. I come to the topic of religious trauma as both witness and survivor of religiously justified physical, emotional, and spiritual abuse in fundamentalist Evangelicalism, whose faith and spiritual practice is deeply shaped by the ongoing effects of trauma. Because my own experience is bound up with the stories of others that are not mine to share, I do not draw explicitly on it in this work. Yet, it inevitably shapes my thinking on the topics discussed, for better and for worse.

Finally, I must acknowledge the risk of addressing religious trauma at this particular historical moment. As I complete revisions, war between Israel and Palestine and the humanitarian crisis it has created in Gaza is being used as the pretext for a swell of antisemitism and Islamophobia around the world. Analysis of religious trauma in communities already subject to hatred could be misappropriated to reinforce harmful stereotypes. This risk is intensified because I write about Islam and Judaism as a religious outsider. Yet victims and survivors in these communities deserve to have their voices heard. Throughout this text I strive to center the voices of survivors and activists from within each religious tradition as "benevolent testifiers" – as those who testify in order to reform rather than destroy (De Cruz 2020: 8), while also acknowledging the practical and epistemic rationality of decisions to leave religion in the wake of religious trauma. Furthermore, no case of abuse presented in this Element should be taken as representative of the tradition as a whole.

1 Trauma and the Human Person

With the rise of the #metoo movement inaugurated by Tarana Burke, the frequency of mass shootings, widely available online-footage of police brutality, and academic debates over the legitimacy of trigger warnings on course syllabi, references to "trauma" are far from anomalous in popular culture or the academy. Yet misconceptions of the nature and effects of trauma are pervasive, and genuinely trauma-informed perspectives and practices remain scarce. Many still operate under the faulty assumption that the truly virtuous and strong among us respond to the obstacles posed by horrific experiences by refusing to allow suffering to get them down. Those whose lives are marked by disability, incapacity, or lasting emotional suffering in the wake of trauma are accused of having a "victim mentality" and choosing self-pity over resilience. This section challenges such misconceptions by describing the causes of trauma, some of the mechanisms that underlie it, and its long-term effects on human agency. It then presents some specific kinds of trauma that are relevant to the discussion of religious trauma: complex trauma, moral injury, and oppression-based trauma.

Although psychological harm associated with intense terror is not new in human experience, the concept of psychological trauma and our current cultural understanding of it is. When first explored under the rubric of "hysteria" by neurologists and those we might anachronistically call early "psychotherapists" such as Jean-Martin Charcot, Pierre Janet, and the early Freud in the late nineteenth century, the phenomenon was primarily associated with women (Herman 2015: 10–20). Although Freud initially believed women's reports of incest and abuse and understood hysteria as an effect of trauma, he later reinterpreted these women's accounts as phantasies arising from sublimated envy and desire (Hacking 1995: 183–209; Herman 2015: 14). According to feminist psychiatrist Judith Herman, this reversal marked the end of the careful psychological study of trauma until it reemerged during World War I. At that point, shell shock, or combat neurosis, gained cultural and political significance, but was understood primarily as the personal weakness of those too lazy or psychologically weak to face the battlefield. Psychiatric treatment often involved electric shock and aggressive emotional shaming, in some cases as a genuine attempt to "cure" the defective soldiers and in others to make the suffering of "malingering" greater than the suffering of warfare (Fassin and Rechtman 2009: 43–50; Herman 2015: 20–28).

Our current understanding of trauma as a normal psychological response to unbearable circumstances and as a psychological wound comparable to physical trauma began to emerge only after World War II when the holocaust became the dominant frame of reference for the psychological and cultural rift of trauma. According to sociologists of trauma Didier Fassin and Richard Rechtman, "the notions of malingering, cowardice, selfishness, overdeveloped narcissism, secondary gains, class interest – all the stigmas attached to traumatic neurosis, could not be applied to these people in striped pajamas who were emerging directly from hell. An entirely different paradigm was called for" (Fassin and Rechtman 2009: 71). In the years following Vietnam, second-wave feminists worked to bring attention to the traumatic experiences of women and children in a patriarchal world, helping to expand the concept of trauma to include the psychic wounds of any encounter with unimaginable horror.

Today our understanding of trauma is informed by work in a number of different research programs. Trauma Theology and the small, but emerging, literature in philosophy of trauma are both deeply informed by "trauma studies," which adopts the resources of psychoanalysis and literary theory to understand the impact of trauma on "the self" in a number of interdisciplinary contexts. Within the psychological sciences, one can focus on the phenotypic manifestations of post-traumatic stress disorder (henceforth PTSD) described in the manuals that govern psychiatric diagnosis such as the *DSM-5* or the ICD-11, on the neurobiological mechanisms of post-traumatic distress and their embodied manifestations, such as work by people like the best-selling authors Bessel Van Der Kolk and Peter Levine, or on treatment of trauma in clinical contexts. Each of these research programs offers unique and valuable insights on which I draw throughout this Element while giving pride of place to the first-person narratives and lived-experiences of trauma survivors.

1.1 The Nature of Trauma

1.1.1 Traumatic Experience

Traumatic experience is notoriously difficult to define, both because of the broad range of possible human experience and because the level of distress an experience causes depends partially on subjective appraisal (Brison 2002: 31; Courtois and Ford 2015: 14). In a broad sense, psychological trauma is anything that overwhelms an individual's usual capacity to process and respond to threats. Judith Herman describes it as a moment in which "the victim is rendered helpless by overwhelming force ... Traumatic events overwhelm the ordinary systems of care that give people a sense of control, connection, and meaning" (Herman 2015: 33). She goes on to say that "[t]raumatic events are extraordinary, not because they occur rarely, but rather because they overwhelm the ordinary human adaptions to life" (Herman 2015: 33, emphasis added). While the *DSM-5* (the *Diagnostic and Statistical Manual of Mental Disorders*, 5th edition) is controversial and limited by its aims and goals, it is currently the primary tool used to diagnose mental disorders in the United States. As such, it is a gatekeeper for insurance coverage, disability benefits, and accommodations at work and in education. For the purpose of a PTSD diagnosis, the *DSM-5* defines traumatic experience as "exposure to actual or threatened death, serious injury, or sexual violence" that is directly experienced, witnessed in person, learned of having occurred to a loved one, or the details of which one is exposed to repeatedly, such as in the case of emergency first responders and psychotherapists (American Philosophical Association 2013: 271). It includes things like violent assault, car accidents, life-threatening natural disasters, intimate-partner violence, child abuse and neglect, incarceration as a prisoner of war, concentration camps, and torture.

1.1.2 Post-traumatic Distress

Exposure to horrors can cause psychological harm that endures long after the experience itself has ended and physical injuries have healed. The *DSM-5* divides the symptoms of PTSD into four primary categories: intrusion symptoms, avoidance behaviors, negative alterations in mood and cognition, and arousal symptoms, with an additional sub-type for the dissociative symptoms of depersonalization and derealization (a sense that events are happening to someone else or that they are distant or unreal). These four categories include things like intrusive memories, persistent nightmares of a traumatic event, hypervigilance, hyperarousal, heightened startle response, memory loss, (unconscious or intentional) avoidance of situations or symbols associated with the trauma, depression, anxiety, chronic shame, flattened affect, and changes in beliefs about the (un)safety and (in)justice of the world, among others (American Philosophical Association 2013: 272). While PTSD tends to be conceptualized as a fear-based response to the threat of annihilation, a recent review article found that, for a subset of people suffering from PTSD, shame rather than fear is the primary response to trauma. Experiencing shame, whether resulting from attribution of blame to the self for the experience or from one's symptoms in its aftermath, according to some theorists, prohibits integration of the traumatic memory into one's identity, thereby preventing recovery. Shame's pathogenic impact appears particularly salient in the wake of chronic interpersonal violence due to the social subordination, powerlessness, and lack of control commonly experienced in these relational and traumatic occurrences. Many have proposed that the loss of wholeness, integrity, and humiliation experienced in relational trauma is also more likely to generate intense feelings of shame rather than fear (Saraiya and Lopez-Castro 2016).

Advances in neuroscience provide insight into the underlying mechanisms of post-traumatic symptoms. The human body responds to perceived threats first via the autonomic (involuntary or unconscious) nervous system, particularly the thalamus, amygdala, and limbic system, which triggers a fight, flight, or freeze response, and milliseconds later via the medial prefrontal cortex (MPC), where rational evaluation takes place (der Kolk 2015; Gonda et al. 2022). Under normal conditions, a stress response and the resulting increase in cortisol levels, heart-rate, and respiration is adaptive, increasing capacity to respond to threats. But when a threat is overwhelming, ongoing, or unescapable, these systems may not return to baseline, and chronic stress results in long-term changes in the brain, such as a reduction in volume of the hippocampus (an organ associated with memory encoding and emotional processing), atrophy of the MPC, increased activity of the amygdala, and reduced levels of the neurotransmitter serotonin. Changes in the hippocampus and amygdala may be responsible for an increase in sensation-based memories (memories felt in the body as opposed to something more akin to viewing a reel "in the mind's eye"), traumatic amnesia, and conditioned fear responses in trauma survivors, while decrease in serotonin levels "may play a role in increased startle reaction, hypervigilance, impulsivity, as well as intrusive traumatic memories" (Gonda et al. 2022: 2). However, neurobiology is not a one-way street where neurological changes simply produce certain emotions, cognitions, and behaviors. These very emotions, cognitions, and behaviors also have neurobiological results. While the causal direction is not always clear, it is probably best to understand the mind and brain as involving a complex set of mutually reinforcing feedback loops. While the neurobiological response to a threat produces certain bodily changes and mental events, the cognitions and emotions a survivor experiences and engages in also impact the brain at a biological level. For example, the review mentioned earlier claims that "shame after trauma has been associated with biological responses, suggestive of an innate reaction to social degradation in traumatic situations that can elicit the cardinal biopsychosocial symptoms of PTSD" (Saraiya and Lopez-Castro 2016: 2). Furthermore, satisfying the formal criteria for a PTSD diagnosis is not a precondition that legitimates post-traumatic suffering. "The research is clear that the consequences of trauma extend far beyond PTSD symptoms to include depression, other anxiety symptoms, substance use, physical health problems, alexithymia, dissociation, and emotion regulation difficulties" (Goldsmith et al. 2014: 119).

In the field of trauma studies, psychic trauma is often conceptualized as an experience so fundamentally horrifying as to be both ineffable and incomprehensible, even to the individual who experiences it. The horror of trauma can never be fully grasped by the experiencing subject or communicated to others using normal conceptual resources of human language. Some theorize that the inability to grasp and articulate the full experience of trauma is why trauma remains and reemerges in intrusive memory, hypervigilance, and altered relationships to the world. This re-experiencing is thought to be the mind's attempt to make sense of what is incomprehensible. As a result, the wound remains in the individual psyche that the community is called, but never fully able, to bear witness to. Cathy Caruth writes that this "trauma seems to be much more than a pathology, or the simple illness of a wounded psyche: it is always the story of a wound that cries out, that addresses us in the attempt to tell us of a reality or truth that is not otherwise available" (Caruth 1996: 4). Shelly Rambo also draws on this idea in her theological account of trauma:

> Trauma is an open wound. For those who survive trauma, the experience of trauma can be likened to a death. But the reality is that death has not ended; instead it persists. The experience of survival is one in which life, as it once was, cannot be retrieved. However, the promise of life ahead cannot be envisioned . . . Without witnessing to what does not go away, to what remains, theology fails to provide sufficient account of redemption. (2010: 7–8)

It is important to note, however, that not everyone who experiences a traumatic event, even the very same traumatic event, will have the same psychological response to it. Several factors influence a victim's vulnerability to post-traumatic distress. These include the nature, severity, and duration of the traumatic experience; biological vulnerabilities such as genetic pre-dispositions, previous illness, and prior mental health; family dynamics and social support; and larger sociopolitical factors. Only 10–20 percent of those who endure a single-event traumatic experience are likely to develop PTSD as defined by the *DSM-5*, while for those who experience ongoing or repetitive traumatic experiences the risk increases to between 33 and 75+ percent (Courtois and Ford 2015: 15).

1.1.3 Post-traumatic Distress and the Self

The effects of trauma reach beyond the bounds of one's own body. We know, believe, love, and survive, or not, within a community. When one's community violates the trust put in it, as happens in interpersonal trauma, the victim does not simply change the way she thinks and feels. The victim may lose her community, her relationships, and indeed her very sense of self. Even when the trauma is not interpersonal, the impact on the self and one's meaning-making capacities also affects one's relationships and place in community. As Judith Herman puts it, "[t]raumatic events have primary effects not only on the psychological structures of the self but also on the systems of attachment and meaning that link the individual and community . . . [they can] destroy the beliefs that one can be oneself in relation to others . . . [Traumatized individuals can] lose their trust in themselves, in other people, and in God" (2015: 51, 56).

One important way that the self is theorized to depend on others is in virtue of its narrative constitution. When narrative theorists speak of the narrative self, there are a number of different things that they can mean. The strongest claim is that one's personal identity, understood in a strong metaphysical sense, is constituted by the narratives that one constructs of oneself in cooperation with one's community (Ricœur 1992; Lindemann 2001). A weaker ontological view holds that human persons have identities – as something distinct from numerical identity – and they are constituted by a narrative (Rea 2022). For Michael Rea, one's narrative identity is what and who others would come to understand one to be by listening perceptively to one's autobiography (i.e., the perceptive listener may draw conclusions that the autobiographer has not and might not even endorse). The various selves we have arise out of such identities. Within the framework of narrative therapy, psychotherapists sometimes frame one's sense of self as a psychologically significant construct constituted by a narrative. Many psychotherapists believe the coherence of the narrative self to be crucial to our well-being. Dan McAdams writes,

> The stories we construct to make sense of our lives are fundamentally about our struggle to reconcile who we imagine we were, are, and might be in our heads and bodies with who we are, and might be in social contexts . . . The self comes to terms with society through narrative identity. (McAdams 2008: 242–243)

This is relevant for our understanding of trauma. The stories we tell about ourselves, to ourselves and our communities, depend in part on the conceptual resources available to us within a social context. Even the social scripts and the narrative tropes that dominate within a culture will strongly influence which life events and which interpretations of them appear most salient to us. Our concepts are never "singular, individual or simply subjective, never outside the social, but have shared or intersubjective meaning within a cultural nexus of power and knowledge" (Brown and Augusta-Scott 2007: ix). If trauma has the ineffable and incomprehensible quality described earlier, then we may lack the conceptual resources necessary to fully narrate the traumatic experience and incorporate it into their narrative identity or sense of self. Furthermore, as we explore in Section 3, communities may intentionally avoid developing those resources and the knowledge that they would mediate. As a result, the narrative self we can construct following trauma may be distorted and truncated in harmful ways. Trauma does more than merely change our brain, our nervous system, and our propositional attitudes. It can fundamentally shape who we are to ourselves and to others and who we can conceive of ourselves as becoming.

Jointly, the symptoms of post-traumatic distress form a web of physical sensations, emotional states, cognitive attitudes, and relationships that is the phenomenal experience of post-traumatic distress. Some survivors describe this experience as a fragmentation of the self – an inability to integrate past and present into a coherent narrative, to fully inhabit one's body, to cope with the world, or to imagine a future that includes oneself (Brison 2002: 68). Susan Brison describes her phenomenal experience in the wake of a brutal rape and attempted murder in the follow way:

> I was no longer the same person I had been before the assault, and one of the ways in which I seemed changed was that I had a different relationship to my body. My body was now perceived as the enemy ... but ... body and mind had become nearly indistinguishable. My mental state (typically depression) felt physiological, like lead in my veins, while my physical state (frequently, incapacitation by fear and anxiety) was the incarnation of a cognitive and emotional paralysis resulting from shattered assumptions about my safety in the world. The symptoms of PTSD gave the lie to the latent dualism that still informs society's most prevalent attitude to trauma, namely, that victims should buck up, put the past behind them, and get on with their lives. My hypervigilance, heightened startle response, insomnia, and the other PTSD symptoms were no more psychological, if that is taken to mean under my conscious control, than were my heart rate and blood pressure. (Brison 2002: 44)

For others, there is no self prior to trauma to be fragmented, lost, or re-narrated. For those who face trauma from their earliest existence, theirs is a self formed in trauma. Childhood may be structured by attempts to avoid harm or appease an abuser, by guilt and shame over failure in that endeavor, by ongoing fear and dread, or by the compulsion to reenact trauma through imaginative play or destructive relationships. For some, post-traumatic distress looks like explosive anger and irritability, inability to hold down a job, or to enter fully into intimate relationships. The survivor may find "herself caught between extremes of amnesia or of reliving the trauma, between floods of intense overwhelming feeling and arid states of no feeling at all, between irritable, impulsive and complete inhibition of action" (Herman 2015: 47). For many, no aspect of the self emerges from trauma unscathed.

1.1.4 Capacities, Compulsion, and Agency

Trauma can also shape the self by undermining the survivor's capacity for morally responsible agency. The impact of mental disorder on agency and moral responsibility is both complex and highly controversial. Accounts of the connection between agency and trauma are also fraught with risk. To attribute agency where it is absent leads to victim-blaming. To deny it where it is present does further harm to survivors by contributing to harmful stereotypes of people with post-traumatic distress symptoms as "crazy," weak, or incompetent. In this section I suggest that some symptoms of post-traumatic distress can sometimes undermine conditions for morally responsible agency, and that some social contexts can sometimes enhance them. Whether such conditions are met for particular survivors may be difficult or impossible to ascertain, not only for an observer, but even for the subject herself, as the limits of our control over our own mental states and behaviors are not always transparent to us. Throughout the discussion, I assume for the sake of argument that the following two criteria are necessary conditions of morally responsible agency: the ability to recognize moral reasons and the ability to respond to moral reasons.

The empirical research on, and first-person testimony about, post-traumatic distress offer strong evidence that its symptoms are often not under the individual's direct, conscious control. The survivor no more chooses to duck when a car backfires than they choose for their heart to beat. As such, the symptoms of post-traumatic distress can constrain what someone is able to do (as in restriction of range of affect) or limit what one is able to refrain from doing (as in heightened startle response or intrusive memories). In these circumstances the condition may constitute either a moral excuse or a moral exemption, depending on one's views of moral responsibility (Watson 1987). In the former case, the individual still bears a moral obligation but is not blameworthy or is less blameworthy than they might otherwise be for failing to satisfy it. In the latter case, the individual does not bear the moral obligation at all because the agent doesn't have the capacities necessary for moral responsibility in that case. Because post-traumatic stress, as other mental disorders, usually does not completely undermine agency or autonomy, I focus on cases of excuse.

Many symptoms of trauma involve affective experience. We do not often think of emotions, even the moral emotions, as something we choose to engage in, even though emotions can be responsive to reasons and apt or not. It is apt to be anxious before one's bar exam but not apt to feel ashamed of having been sexually assaulted (even if understandable). Yet, such emotions are not as easily responsive to reasons as, say, propositional attitudes. Coming to see that a belief is false is usually sufficient for rejecting the belief. And, at times, emotions respond similarly. Sometimes, one need only discover that one's fear is unwarranted for the fear to disappear (e.g., the snake on the path is really a stick). At others, one can continue to feel an emotion even after one realizes that one's feeling is unwarranted (e.g., "I know I am not to blame for the assault, but I still feel shame."). Many of the symptoms of post-traumatic distress are of this sort and can have a profound impact on what one is able to do and to refrain from doing. In a panic attack, it may be impossible or exceedingly difficult not to hyperventilate or to maintain a calm conversation with one's co-worker. In hypervigilance, it may be impossible or extremely difficult to wear noise-canceling headphones that would help one to focus but also leave one feeling vulnerable. Sometimes such impacts are global (i.e., it impacts the subject as a whole person, as flashbacks that "overtake" one's entire consciousness). Others are local (i.e., impacting only one aspect of their experience or self, as in loss of affective range). Some impacts are episodic (i.e., happening for short bursts of time, as in intrusive memories or panic attacks), while others are stable (i.e., remaining more or less fixed for long periods of time, as depression or generalized anxiety). Some are predictable (e.g., intrusive memories triggered by certain stimuli), while others are unpredictable (e.g., nightmares).

Finally, these impacts are ecologically contextual (Timpe 2019). Kevin Timpe argues that not only the agency of disabled individuals, but human agency in general depends on one's social and structural environment. What someone suffering from post-traumatic distress is able to do and to refrain from doing is not only a function of their body and mind but of the structural and relational features of their environment. Whether a survivor of a school shooting can pay attention to a lecture or is distracted by their hypervigilant monitoring of the hallway for potential threats may be a function of whether or not the classroom door is closed and locked during class. Whether the depressed survivor is able to get out of bed may depend on whether their partner is willing to help them through their morning routine. That is, their agency may be bolstered or further impaired by the structure of their community. While some symptoms of trauma may be incapacitating in the very same sense as physical paralysis, others are incapacitating in the weaker sense of making things more difficult than they would otherwise be. This explains how survivors of trauma generally maintain robust agency in some areas while it is impaired in others in ways that may constitute moral excuse and warrant accommodations and care from their communities.

There are also ways in which responding to trauma and coping with its effects sometimes impart skills that enhance agency. While hypervigilance is a heavy burden on the nervous system, hypervigilant people may be the first to recognize and respond to a threat. People who have experienced abuse are often able to recognize signs of abuse that other people miss. Survivor communities often have nuanced and sophisticated systems of care that can serve as models for the social scaffolding of dependent agency (Piepizna-Samarasinha 2018). Survivors often know how to dissociate, which is a learnable skill sometimes helpful in recovery and in spiritual practice (see Section 5). In her book *Trauma Magic* Clementine Morrigan argues that "the embodied experiences of trauma are one means with which to resist violence, and that embodied experiences of trauma can offer new ways of being the world" (2021: 19). This however should not be used as justification for, or glorification of, violence or suffering, or for thinking that the badness of violence can be outweighed by the benefits it imparts. Morrigan continues, "I insist on the simultaneous importance of work to end violence, and desiring the difference of the disabled embodiment that is trauma" (19) and goes on to cite Eli Clare, who writes, "when the woman whose body has been shaped by military pollution declares, 'I hate the military and love my body,' she is saying something brand new and deeply complex" (Clare 2014: 15, cited in Morrigan 2021: 29). This is the complexity that Morrigan, Piepizna-Samarasinha, and others argue we need with respect to the effects of trauma. Some effects may be either inherently or relatively (to the person) bad, while others may be inherently or relatively (to the person) good. And both the good and the bad, where they exist, may be bound up in complex ways in the lived experience of the survivor. No single evaluation can capture this complexity.

Popular culture paints the person who "bounces back" or is especially resilient in the wake of trauma as morally superior to those who do not, but personal merit has little to do with one's vulnerability to the long-term effects of trauma. The symptoms of trauma can be incapacitating regardless of what one believes or does in the wake of the experience, even though how one chooses to exercise agency in the wake of trauma is not insignificant for who one becomes in its wake. While it is important to avoid painting survivors as passive, helpless, or impotent in the process of recovery, the information provided in this section suggests that we should reject any simplistic attribution of praise or blame to an individual's experience of post-traumatic distress. There is also a danger that a helpful category like psychic trauma can become a totalizing narrative for suffering (Fassin and Rechtman 2009). Trauma is just one form of suffering in a world rife with pain. The suffering of trauma should not be taken as special or ultimate in any way, as if those who suffer trauma are more (or less) deserving of moral attention than those who suffer in other ways. Neither should we take the symptoms of post-traumatic distress as the proof of the reality or degree of suffering that someone experiences. While intensity and duration are important factors in the statistical likelihood of experiencing post-traumatic symptoms, many people who suffer unspeakably do not develop clinical PTSD. This does not mean that the accident, abuse, torture, or disaster was less bad or less in need of social and spiritual attention.

1.2 Some Varieties of Trauma

The previous section offers a general account of post-traumatic distress. But given the breadth of possible human experience, different kinds of trauma tend to have uniquely identifiable impacts. In this section, I provide an overview of three particular kinds of trauma that may overlap in significant ways with religious trauma.

1.2.1 Complex Trauma

The ICD-11 (International Classification of Diseases, 11th edition) defines Complex Post-Traumatic Stress Disorder as a disorder that "may develop following exposure to an event or series of events of an extremely threatening or horrific nature, most commonly prolonged or repetitive events from which escape is difficult or impossible (e.g., torture, slavery, genocide campaigns, prolonged domestic violence, repeated childhood sexual or physical abuse)." The diagnostic criteria are the same as the ICD's criteria for PTSD but include three additional categories of diagnostic criteria:

> [S]evere and persistent 1) problems in affect regulation [examples include heightened emotional reactivity to minor stressors, violent outbursts, reckless or self-destruct behavior, dissociative symptoms when under stress, and emotional numbing, particularly the inability to experience pleasure or positive emotions]; 2) beliefs about oneself as diminished, defeated or worthless, accompanied by feelings of shame, guilt or failure related to the traumatic event; and 3) difficulties in sustaining relationships and in feeling close to others. (World Health Organization n.d.)

Complex trauma is especially likely to arise in childhood, because children are especially dependent and relatively politically powerless, and therefore especially vulnerable to severe and long-term abuse. For similar reasons, disabled and elderly people are also at elevated risk. The large, long-term Adverse Childhood Experience Project demonstrates that in addition to the psychological and emotional symptoms described in the previous section, those who experience childhood trauma are orders of magnitude more likely than their peers to suffer from chronic health problems, to end up in abusive relationships, to struggle with substance abuse, and to attempt or die by suicide (Felitti et al. 1998; Harris 2018).

Conceiving of some especially severe and long-lasting forms of trauma as a separate category is important for some psychologists because such experiences tend to result in symptoms that are pervasive in the individual's fundamental sense of self (often resulting in misdiagnoses as dissociative identity disorder, borderline personality disorder, and bipolar disorder) and more resistant to treatment. Emmanuel Tanay, a psychiatrist who worked with survivors of the Holocaust, observed that "the psychopathology [of complex trauma] may be hidden in the characterological changes that are manifest only in disturbed object relationships and attitudes towards work, the world, man and God" (Herman 2015: 120).

Complex trauma is important for an analysis of religious trauma because of the role that religion plays in the life of religious believers. For many, the religious worldview functions as a comprehensive doctrine – a lens through which the rest of the world is interpreted and responded to. Furthermore, hierarchical structures, justified within a religious context and mirrored within the familial system, can create an environment where totalitarian control is exercised at the community or family level. Although theocracies and high-control new religious movements are two forms of totalitarian religion, such control can also arise within more mainstream religious contexts when religious leaders exercise disproportionate control over members. Because it is difficult to leave a community that forms so much of one's identity and social support, those who find themselves under religiously traumatizing conditions often struggle to leave, and are subjected to the abuse for long periods of time, creating the conditions for complex traumatization. Furthermore, religious views are often passed down generationally. Add to this the level of physical and epistemic vulnerability of children, and we can see why many cases of religious trauma qualify as complex trauma.

1.2.2 Moral Injury

The construct of moral injury emerged originally in the psychological literature to account for the experiences of veterans whose consciences had been violated by their own and others' actions in combat situations. It is defined as "the lasting psychological, biological, spiritual, behavioral, and social [harm]" to oneself that may result from "perpetrating, failing to prevent, or bearing witness to acts that transgress deeply held moral beliefs and expectations" (Litz et al. 2009: 697). It is often divided into two categories: cases resulting from the action or inaction of the individual themself (e.g., perpetrating or failing to prevent harm) or cases resulting from witnessing the action or inaction of others, usually authority figures or those with whom one bears a significant bond (e.g., betrayal by trusted others or witnessing violence) (Barnes et al. 2019: 99). The harm in view is neither that of becoming a morally worse agent or of having one's capacity to exercise moral agency undermined, but rather the negative repercussions of violations of one's conscience. Nor does the concept include any evaluation of the moral perspective from which an individual finds actions deeply morally distressing. As a result, one could not only claim but actually *be* morally injured by their own or others' morally good or neutral actions if those actions violate one's own deeply held moral beliefs. Although this may initially seem counterintuitive (how could someone be injured by doing something good?), it seems true that the psychological distress and feelings of guilt or shame that something causes arise from subjective moral appraisal rather than from some objectively true moral perspective. However, the construct entails that the distinction between moral injury resulting from one's own behavior and injury resulting from witnessing others' behavior will not neatly track who, if anyone, is at *moral fault.*[1]

While both post-traumatic distress and moral injury follow from events broadly categorized as "trauma," post-traumatic distress is seen as arising from the fear-causing experiences that trigger a fight, flight, or freeze response, while moral injury is seen as arising from the *moral* contours of the experience. It is characterized by moral emotions such as guilt, shame, anger, and grief. Symptoms of moral

---

[1] I thank a referee for pushing me to make these implications clearer.

injury may include the symptoms of post-traumatic distress in addition to things like self-harm, hopelessness, disrupted relationships, and negative shifts in spirituality (Griffin et al. 2019: 1). This category is significant for thinking about religious trauma because communities and survivors often bear witness to spiritual abuse and may experience spiritual and social pressure to violate their own moral and religious values in service of abusers or the status quo.

1.2.3 Oppression-based Trauma

Recent research has begun to show not only that members of socially marginalized groups experience a higher frequency of PTSD, even when they report lower numbers of traumatic experiences, but that they often present with symptoms of PTSD without experiencing "trauma" as defined by the *DSM*. As a result, some researchers believe that chronic, lower-level harms that constitute a threat to one's sense of self and social belonging can produce symptoms as severe as threats of death or serious injury. In response to these findings, a small number of scholars have begun working on a constellation of constructs I here call "oppression-based trauma," although the phenomenon continues to be under-researched and is currently discussed under a number of different terms (Root 1992; Carter 2007; Szymanski and Balsam 2011; Holmes et al. 2016; Watson et al. 2016). First developed by Maria Root as "insidious trauma," Root describes it as "characterized by multiple lower level, harmful events that occur throughout an individual's lifetime" and "inherently identity-based and directed at those with marginalized identities by persons who hold power and privilege" (Watson, et al. 2016: 656). Experiences may include persistent discrimination, low-level violence, objectification, microaggressions, and other manifestations of oppression and social marginalization. Although one can be privileged in one context while marginalized in another, because oppression-based trauma results from the cumulative effect of a large number of "small" harms, it is most likely to occur in cases where oppression is systematic across many contexts within one's experience. However, the personal significance of those context(s) will likely be relevant to the degree of impact.[2]

Given that those who are marginalized by the broader society have also, historically, been marginalized within many religious communities, we should expect for some cases of religious trauma to also be oppression-based. Furthermore, because spirituality tends to be a central source of meaning-making, marginalization in religious spaces that is not replicated in the broader society may be more likely to result in trauma than other highly localized forms of marginalization.

---

[2] I thank a referee for encourage me to elaborate on the significance of context.

2 Religious Trauma and Religious Selves

Perhaps one reason the public is currently mesmerized by stories of religious trauma is their apparent incongruence. Religion purports to offer something nourishing and true–something that will bring people closer to God, their fellow human, and the universe. And it often does. Revolutionaries and quiet helpers the world over have been motivated by their religious convictions. Individuals often find deep comfort in their religious beliefs, practices, and communities. This makes it all the more horrifying when religion harms rather than heals. Throughout this Element I assume that religion is neither inherently good nor bad. Religions make claims about reality that may be either true or false; recommend practices and attitudes that can be healthy, spiritually nourishing, or damaging; and foster moral visions that can be good or bad. Indeed, it is partly because some religion, or aspects of many, might be true and good, and because spirituality is an important system of meaning-making, that undermining a person's religious and spiritual agency in the ways explored in this Element is such a fundamental violation.

In this section, I begin by examining a series of case studies of religious abuse across Judaism, Christianity, and Islam. I then outline the nascent empirical research on the phenomenon, and finally provide a general characterization of religious trauma and its effects on spiritual agency. Readers should be aware that this section includes discussion of sexual, physical, and emotional abuse; racism; and anti-LGBTQ+ religious teachings. Discussion of each kind of abuse is clearly labeled, and readers wishing to avoid them may skip to section 2.2 with minimal loss of comprehension.

2.1 Case Studies

Analytic philosophy of religion has sometimes been conducted in a highly abstract and disembodied way. Although such methodology can produce valuable insight, it often fails to capture what is at stake for real people who experience suffering and tends to obscures important aspects of the human experience about which philosophy of religion should have something to say. As an alternative Mikel Burley recommends drawing on "thick descriptions" of religious "lifeways" found in ethnography and works of literary fiction, where the philosopher confronts the "other" in all the complexity of their spiritual and religious way of life (Burley 2020). In that spirit, I here draw extensively on thick descriptions of religious trauma from qualitative psychological studies, memoirs, survivor community blogs, and truth and reconciliation projects. Such narratives may help us to avoid objectifying sufferers by turning them into mere abstract entities–Person A and Person B–for the purposes of philosophical theorizing and help us to get a better sense of what religious trauma is like from the inside. However, lurid description can both facilitate an objectifying form of voyeurism and (re)traumatize readers. This section aims to balance faithfulness to experience with respect for the people who have lived it.

2.1.1 Clergy Sexual Abuse in Catholicism

Klaudia, a Polish Catholic woman, was seventeen when she was sexually assaulted by a priest who ministered to the youth in her community. When interviewed about the experience ten years later, she displayed visible distress and struggled to continue discussion. She recounted not only feeling that God was disgusted and repulsed by her for "allowing the abuse to happen," but that she had experienced God's presence "wove[n] into the very experience of abuse." God's presence was made palpable to her during the assault in part by a cross the priest wore around his neck, an oath to God he forced her to swear afterward, and the mass he performed and which she attended mere hours later. She described experiencing this divine presence not as a source of comfort or as a sympathetic witness, but as a severe, judgmental observer of her shame and guilt. She describes "a sense of having hurt Jesus by not being able to stop the abuser, because God saw it all and must have been angry at her" (Prusak and Schab 2022: 56). She says,

> I didn't take Communion [at the mass following the abuse] . . . I couldn't. I felt strong internal . . . ehm . . . confusion? As if everything inside me was upset . . . But God knew about it, didn't He? He must have been angry at me at the time . . . And after all that happened he, I mean the priest, told me to swear to God that I wouldn't tell anyone!" (55)

Klaudia reported feeling no resentment toward God, either for his anger or for allowing the abuse to occur. Rather, she shared having difficulty reconciling herself to the fact that God created her as a sexual being–something that she has come to experience as a source of evil.

> You know, it seems I transferred this to myself in a way by passing a judgment on my body. For me, sexuality is associated with . . . well, with great evil. My sexuality is simply evil! I can't come to terms with the fact that . . . well, it was God who created it . . . I feel dirty for every manifestation of my sexuality . . . (54)

Not only her sense of relationship with God and with the church, but also her sense of self as an embodied sexual being are deeply harmed by the assault.

When William was in the fifth or sixth grade, the priest to whom he had gone for confession held him forcibly against his body and kissed him repeatedly on the mouth while he did his best to escape. In the years following, William struggled with deep confusion about what had happened to him, turned to alcohol to cope, and attempted suicide. As an adult he was final able to report the abuse. The diocese initially agreed to pay for his counseling, but soon backed out of their promise and eventually offered him a sum of money to lie about the nature of their previous commitments. Reflecting on the experience he says,

> As a boy, when I asked for the sacrament of reconciliation, I came with defenses down and total trust in Catholic Christian goodness to help me heal, and was instead betrayed, abused, and left powerless. Later, as a man, I did the same when I approached the Diocese of Peoria, coming to them defenses down, never using a lawyer, and trusting that surely their professed Catholic Christian compassion and goodness would lead to healing. Instead, just like I was spiritually raped in the confessional as a boy, they bullied me with lawyers, wanting me powerless, accepting terms that benefitted their interests ... This was trust-shattering, spiritually disillusioning revictimization at the merciless, selfpreserving hands of the Diocese of Peoria. (Office of the Illinois Attorney General 2023: 439, 443)

2.1.2 Sexual Harassment and Spiritual Abuse in a Sufi Community

The first time Aisha met the *Shaykh* (a religious leader) in her community, he touched her on her head and back, despite a religious prohibition against doing so. Aisha initially concluded that this was a part of *ruqya* (a ritual of healing). However, at subsequent encounters, he began asking her invasive questions about her sexual history and kissed her face and "all over" without her consent (Qasim 2019). Afterwards, members of the community used theological explanations to minimize the experience and try to convince her that she was the one at fault for telling others about her discomfort with these violations. The *Shaykh* initially rebutted her account by claiming that she had misinterpreted his fatherly gestures of comfort, that he no longer experienced any sexual desire, and that she was not beautiful enough to pose a temptation anyway. At other times, he claimed that his action was part of *haqiqa* (one of the four stages in the Sufi path, characterized by mystical knowledge obtained by communion with God) and that her reaction demonstrated that she knew nothing of this spiritual stage. He further claimed that she had a bad character and was engaging in backbiting by talking about the experience. This treatment led Aisha to apologize to her harasser and to seek forgiveness from God. She writes:

> I went to my room, feeling I had committed a sin; I felt in physical pain the whole night because I thought I committed a big sin of backbiting a wali [saint]. My friends came and tried to calm me down and told me to apologize to him the next morning ...

The isolation caused me to become consumed by guilt and fear, especially after they came to my hometown to make sure I never told anyone. The stress also caused me to lose a lot of weight. I looked thin and very pale during their visit . . .

I went back home feeling heavy with all this guilt I carried around. I kept asking Allah to forgive me for questioning the Shaykh and even accusing him of something like that. (Qasim 2019)

Aisha is harmed not only as a sexual being and not only as a knower pressured to doubt her ability to recognize sexual harassment, but as a Sufi Muslim whose understanding of the path to union with God is coopted into a justification for abuse.

2.1.3 Intimate Partner Sexual Violence in a Haredi Community

Devorah, a devout Haredi woman, was sexually violated by her husband. She reports being forced to have intercourse with him during her period of ritual menstrual impurity. According to Jewish law, a woman is not to have physical contact with her husband during menstruation and until seven days after the cessation of bleeding and she has immersed herself in a *mikve taharah* (ritual bath). Because following this prohibition is deeply spiritually significant to Devorah, the coercion is not only a sexual assault, but a forced violation of her deeply held religious values, a form of moral injury. Although according to Jewish law, the perpetrator of such abuse is the one morally and spiritually responsible for the violation, Devorah still reports feeling "terrible," "full of shame," and being "unable to accept herself." She describes experiencing herself as "far from the Almighty and unworthy of his love" (Dehan and Levi 2009: 1302). Devorah's relationship with God and her self-perception as a Jewish woman are deeply negatively impacted by this experience in ways that may not be reducible either to the impact of either sexual abuse or moral injury alone.

All four of the victims described here experience the trauma of a sexual violation and the sorts of post-traumatic symptoms that one would expect after any trauma: shame, fear, anxiety, weight loss, suicidality, conflicted relationships with sexuality, and so on. But in each case, their experience includes an additional spiritual violation that continues to shape how they see themselves in relation to the divine, their own spiritual practices, and the religious institution. They perceive themselves as guilty or shameful before the divine, as the object of divine anger, and as separated from God. Klaudia cannot see her sexuality as a gift from a loving God. Aisha is encouraged to doubt her understanding of the Sufi path. And Devorah sees herself as far from the Almighty and unworthy of love. Klaudia is inhibited from receiving the Eucharist, a means of divine grace within her tradition. William is "spiritually disillusioned." All of them experience what

Nicole Dehan and Zipi Levi describe as a destruction of the "inner feeling of spiritual integrity" (2009: 1302).

2.1.4 Homophobic Theology and Shaming in Evangelical Communities

Kyle is a gay, Australian evangelical who was outed for his sexuality at school and forced into Christian conversion therapy. He describes the aftermath as follows:

> That was probably the lowest point that it ever got because it was just a constant barrage of being told that I am horrible, that I am never going to amount to anything in life, and because of this small difference, I will never be considered human, never be considered like everybody else, never be loved, never be accepted, never have a wife. At this point, same-sex marriage was illegal, so I was also struggling with that – if I do this, I'm never going to marry the person I love, never going to have the same rights as everybody else. So that was the lowest it ever got. (Hollier et al. 2022: 282)

In a similar vein, Jarrod Parker describes his experience in church after "failing" to change his sexual orientation:

> I soon found myself even more depressed because I wasn't changing – and even more isolated. My church treated me like I was a disease. People who had been friends stopped speaking to me. I once sat in the second row at church, but I began to feel I had to sit in the very back. (Cockayne, Efird, and Warman 2020: 136)

While some LGBTQIA+ survivors of religious abuse and trauma report feeling loved and accepted by God even while abuse in their churches was ongoing (Tobin and Moon 2020), others report continuing to feel fear and shame before God even after they rejected the theological perspective that harmed them. Lucas describes what Tobin and Moon call the "sacramental shame" (shame that is demanded as the precondition for spiritual belonging) he felt:

> I have all the information that I would need to know that, like, same-sex unions would not be a problem. I can tell you right now I'd probably accept a proposal. I'd have the party [. . .] I'd get to that church [. . . .] I have all the relationship models, I have all the ministry models . . . and I even, like, can sit down and exegete scripture [. . .] So, I mean, I know these things, but, like, it's not satiated. The fear just still hasn't gone away. [. . .] I guess that's the fear [. . .] – not that we get there and there's no God, that we get there, there is a God, and this God is this hateful person with this trident and this long beard and this dress and is, you know, crazy homophobic. (Tobin and Moon 2020: 150–151)

It is notable that Lucas's affective response to God does not align with his intellectual commitments long after escaping a spiritually abusive environment.

He desires to love and trust God, but he is unable to eradicate this deep fear of rejection.

2.1.5 Physical Abuse in Fundamentalist Christianity

Lani Harper describes the religious teaching that formed the background for child-maltreatment in her family:

> [Children] are born sinners, with the innate and persistent duty [*sic*] to sin against their parents. It is an us-versus-them mentality: the children are against us, are going to undermine us, are going to undo us at an elemental level. Consequently, the parents' focus becomes the need to stand firm against their children's "wiles", and to guard themselves against being drawn astray by their children. To be strong and stronger than their children. To resist their children anytime the parents feel pulled against their will, their desires, their instincts. And then to deny their children as they ask for things, in an attempt to show the children, as my father would say, who's boss. With this perspective, every small blunder became magnified under the perception that we were elementally sinful, deliberately devious, manipulative, intentionally-subversive. (Harper 2013a)

Lani endured severe beatings that caused loss of bladder control and extensive bruising as punishment for perceived "sins" such as spilling a glass of milk at the dinner table. Afterward, her father

> made [her] recite a verse or two while pulling [her] clothes back on with trembling fingers. There was a lecture about how this was his God-given duty to show love to [her] and help [her] become less sinful, that [she] deserved more, worse and should be thankful, that this was hard and he didn't like it but it was necessary and in [her] best interests. (Harper 2013b)

At the time of writing, Lani was a thirty-six-year-old wife and mother of three. Yet, eighteen years after leaving the abusive home environment she writes:

> I still remember the humiliation and ferocious anger at being violated on the outside by the beating and on the inside by the changes they sought to force into us, by the association to God and spirituality. It affects me decades later and has thus shaped my views on everything from parenting to God to spirituality, to self-worth and more. (ibid.)

2.1.6 Racism in North American Christianity

Religiously justified racism, up to and including genocide, is so central to American history that one might say that the United States is built upon a foundation of religious trauma. Charles Mills explains how theological constructs facilitated the "conceptual partitioning" of "savages" on one hand and "citizens" or just "men" on the other that is central to the "racial contract" (Mills 1997: 13). In the case of the Spanish conquest of the Americas, acknowledgment of Indigenous people's rationality by Catholic Europeans depended on their acceptance of both the Christian message and Spanish rule, while rejection of either was regarded as proving irrationality and their rightful exclusion from the moral community. This "justified" the Spanish in dispossessing them of land and enslaving them (22). Later, indigenous children in the United States and Canada were forcibly placed in religious boarding schools in an attempt to "civilize" them. Many indigenous Americans had already converted to Christianity, but others still practiced traditional forms of spirituality. Few had assimilated to European culture to the degree that Western authorities deemed necessary.

Vitaline Elsie Jenner was physically and sexually abused at Fort Chipewyan school in Alberta. She recounts being punished for talking to a friend during class by a priest repeatedly stabbing her hand with a headpin, so that she would "feel what Jesus felt on the cross ... feel the same pain" (Truth and Reconciliation Commission 2015: 88). The crucifixion, rather than a symbol of the love of a fellow victim, became for Jenner a horrifying symbol of what she deserved for her normal childhood behavior. Jenner recounts how latter in life she experienced deep shame about her sexually maturing body and about her identity as an indigenous person. She discloses, with tears, that she would do anything, from dying her hair to excessive drinking, to hide and to forget her indigenous identity. Many survivors recall teachers and clergy in boarding schools contrasting the "cleanness" of God and the white teachers with them, the "dirty Indians." They were then made to pray to the "same God that made [them] feel guilty because [they were] ... not very clean person[s]" (86).

Throughout the report on indigenous boarding schools from the Canadian Truth and Reconciliation Commission, we see religious authority figures and representatives of religious communities inflicting abuse in the name of God; notions of atonement and other points of theology weaponized to justify the abuse; and post-traumatic effects that include negative or hindered relationships both with the Christian God and with indigenous spirituality. This spiritual abuse not only caused trauma to individual victims, but inextricably linked spirituality to the genocidal impact of these boarding schools.

The vignettes in this section illustrate some of the diverse ways in which religious trauma can manifest in monotheistic contexts, but they are far from exhaustive, omitting discussion of religious justifications of chattel slavery, the Crusades, marginalization of disabled believers, practices of shunning and excommunication and myriad others. Given my own context in the United States where Christianity has disproportionate social and political power to inflict religious violence and is therefore chief among sinners with respect to religious trauma, the weight of examples presented also reflects this. If I were writing as a Muslim in a Muslim-majority country or a Jewish woman in Israel, the weight of examples would undoubtedly look different.

2.2 Empirical Research on Religious Trauma

Exceptionally little empirical, peer-reviewed research has been done on religious trauma in the psychological sciences. At present, no data on the frequency of religious abuse within any particular religious community or population, or on risk of developing religious trauma or symptoms of PTSD more generally following religious abuse, have been published. However, attention to the topic is growing in promising ways. At the time of writing, I have identified twelve empirical studies – six quantitative and six qualitative – of phenomena that fall broadly into the category of religious trauma. These include three studies on spiritual abuse (Dehan and Levi 2009; Ward 2011; Koch and Edstrom 2022), four on clergy sexual abuse (McLaughlin 1994; Rossetti 1995; Zalcberg 2017; Prusak and Schab 2022), two on anti-LGBTQ+ teachings and conversion therapy in religious contexts (Hollier et al. 2022; Jones et al. 2022), two on "religion-related abuse" broadly defined (Bottoms et al. 1995; Nobakht and Yngvar Dale 2018), and one on religiously motivated physical abuse (Bottoms et al. 2004). Six focus on Christians from an array of traditions (McLaughlin 1994; Rossetti 1995; Ward 2011; Hollier et al. 2022; Koch and Edstrom 2022; Prusak and Schab 2022), three on diverse (but majority Christian) populations (Bottoms et al. 1995; Bottoms et al. 2004; Jones et al. 2022), two on Haredi Jewish communities (Dehan and Levi 2009; Zalcberg 2017), and one on college students in Iran (Nobakht and Yngvar Dale 2018). Given limits of sample size and higher than ideal p-values (this value represents the likelihood of producing a false positive–that is, of mistakenly confirming the hypothesis that a variable is significant), the results of studies should be taken as suggestive rather than conclusive or generalizable.

It is difficult to summarize the central findings of such a diverse array of studies, but I mention a few particularly interesting findings here. Two studies found significantly worse mental health – including higher rates of depression, anxiety, suicidal ideation, and dissociative identity disorder – among survivors of abuse in religious contexts than both the general population and survivors of abuse in nonreligious contexts (Bottoms et al. 1995; Bottoms et al. 2004). For example, "42% of religion-related abuse victims, but only 15% of other victims and 20% of the control group could be classified as clinically depressed" (Bottoms et al. 2004: 104). This may suggest that, all other things being equal, abuse in a religious context is more traumatic than the same kinds of abuse when they occur outside of religion. Of the seven studies (four qualitative and three quantitative) that assessed the impact of religiously or spiritually significant trauma on later engagement in religious practices (such as prayer, reading religious texts, and attending religious services), five reported decreased in engagement in survivors (McLaughlin 1994; Hollier et al. 2022; Jones et al. 2022; Koch and Edstrom 2022; Prusak and Schab 2022). Seven studies found that religious trauma is correlated with a worsened sense of relationship with God (McLaughlin 1994; Rossetti 1995; Dehan and Levi 2009; Hollier et al. 2022; Jones et al. 2022; Koch and Edstrom 2022; Prusak and Schab 2022). And one study showed that those who had been sexually abused by clergy had less trust in God than both those who had not been abused at all and those who had been abused by nonclergy (Rossetti 1995).

While this research is nascent, and causation is notoriously difficult to empirically verify, especially in matters where humans exercise personal agency, what little data we have is highly suggestive of the hypothesis that abuse in a religious or spiritual context amplifies the impact of the abuse and damages relationships to the divine and spiritual community.

2.3 Characterizing Religious Trauma

Clinicians have defined religious trauma in a few different ways, each reflecting important features of the examples provided earlier. Marlene Winell, in her groundbreaking work on religious trauma syndrome, describes religious trauma as the experience of leaving an abusive, controlling, or otherwise physically, psychologically, or emotionally damaging religious group (2011). Her characterization is helpful because it accurately identifies a number of contexts in which religious traumatization is likely to occur, but it is overly narrow in a number of ways. First, the trauma of leaving a religious community is, in principle, separable from other traumas experienced while in the group. One can experience religious trauma and its effects without ever leaving one's religious community. Devorah's story illustrates this. The assault and forced violation of religious law are spiritually traumatic for her even while she remains married to an abusive husband and a part of the Haredi community. Second, religious trauma need not conceptually depend on the religious group being abusive or otherwise damaging. An abusive person might find their way into an otherwise healthy group and inflict religiously significant trauma on people within it. Victims might be religiously traumatized even if the group responded appropriately to their disclosures. Not all forms of trauma arise from interpersonal violence or social structures. For example, one survivor of the abuse of a controlling and manipulative Sufi *Shaykh* describes how his early days in the abusive community involved not only a number of positive mystical experiences, but also some very dark, yet spiritually significant ones: "we interpreted the dark and scary experiences as an important block towards building deep spirituality" (Anonymous 2021). These negative and traumatic experiences were not inflicted by the abuser or any other human person, and it is not clear that they resulted from anything inherently abusive in the religious social structure. They came about in and through private spiritual practice. Thus, Winell's characterization captures an important subset of religious trauma, but is not broad enough to capture all.

Theresa Pasquale, a survivor of religious trauma and a licensed therapist, also offers a characterization of religious trauma in her book *Sacred Wounds: A Path to Healing from Spiritual Trauma*: "any painful experience perpetrated by family, friends, community members, or institutes inside of religion" (Pasquale 2015: 22). While this definition is more expansive, it in turn includes too much. Not all pain is bad for us on the whole. Donating blood is usually mildly painful but not a bad thing to do; having one's abusive behaviors called out may be painful, but it provides the opportunity for growth. Furthermore, even painfully bad experiences do not always rise to the level of inflicting trauma. If everything negative or painful counts as trauma, then the category loses its significance. As described in the first section, current neurobiology suggests that at least many of the symptoms of trauma result from the long-term over-activation of the nervous system's completely healthy response to a threat to life or personal integrity. One of the hallmarks of trauma that distinguishes it from lower-level negative experiences is its remainder and intrusion into one's life and consciousness in the aftermath. Trauma is not something experienced and easily left behind, but something that, without intervention, continues to be experienced, often in ways that lead to a fragmented sense of self and diminished flourishing. Finally, not all genuinely traumatic experiences caused by something or someone in religion will be religiously significant for the survivor. One might be trapped in a collapsed Mosque during an earthquake and be deeply traumatized by the experience, without that trauma being distinctly religiously valanced. Likewise, if one is sexually violated by a clergy member without ever knowing that the perpetrator is a clergy member, the impact of the trauma is unlikely to be specifically religiously significant the way it would be if the perpetrator were one's own priest, pastor, rabbi, or *shaykh*. Therefore, we need a characterization that is broader than Winell's but narrower than Pasquale's.

I doubt that it is possible to provide necessary and sufficient conditions for the phenomenon of religious trauma, both because of the richness and variety of religious traditions and phenomena, and because the very notion of trauma involves not only a particular kind of experience, but one's subjective appraisal of it. However, there are good philosophical and psychological reasons to delineate some common characteristics of paradigmatic cases of it while acknowledging the fuzziness of those boundaries. I suggest that religiously traumatic experiences paradigmatically include the following three characteristics.

1) The traumatic experience has deep religious significance to the individual.
2) It leads to religiously significant post-traumatic distress.
3) The post-traumatic effects have a negative impact on the individual's religious or spiritual life.

A traumatic experience can be religiously significant because the cause of the experience is deeply associated with the religion or because the experience is of some aspect of the religion or one's own religious identity. This might be because the perpetrator plays an important religious role, such as a religious parent, priest, or imam (as in Lori, Devorah, Aisha, Klaudia's, and the children's in indigenous boarding schools cases); because the experience was justified on religious grounds, (e.g., by appeal to a religious text, as in the case of LGBTQ+ Evangelicals); because it is inflicted for religious reasons or as part of religious practices (as in Aisha's case when the *Shaykh* claimed that his violation was a part of *haqiqa*); it arises from negatively valenced mystical or transcendent experiences (as the "dark" spiritual experiences described by the anonymous survivor earlier); or because the individual experiences the event through a deeply religiously significant frame of reference, where the religious framework makes the experience the kind of experience that it is (as in Devorah's case). A Muslim woman whose *hijab* is ripped off by an Islamophobic assailant will not experience this in the same way as a nonreligious person would experience the theft of an ordinary scarf. Even if the material objects are the same, the religious significance of the *hijab* (to both the victim and perpetrator) makes it a religiously significant experience for the *hijab*-wearer but not for the scarf-wearer.

In the past, I have categorized this latter type of case (involve persecution experiences like *hijab*-snatching) as related to, but distinct from, religious trauma because the cause of the experience is not itself religious (Panchuk 2018). Because religious persecution is often interpreted in the Christian tradition as a badge of honor, and victims and martyrs are highly respected and praised, I did not initially conceive of persecution experiences as something that could undermine one's religious agency, but as something that bolsters it. I believe that was mistaken and that my former perspective demonstrated Christo-centrism and lack of imagination about the ways in which religious persecution might be experienced. Someone who veils out of religious conviction and who is traumatized by an Islamophobic assault may experience the trauma as deeply religiously significant. I hypothesize that the post-traumatic effects may be both more religiously significant and more severe in cases where the individual's own religion plays a causal role in the trauma, because the victim is more likely to internalize the perspective of the abuser and because the victim is more likely to experience a sense of alienation from God and their religious community, but that some level of religiously-valanced trauma may arise in either kind of case. However, this hypothesis would require empirical validation.

Many experiences that satisfy the first characteristic will be cases of spiritual abuse. Like religious trauma, there is no single conceptualization of spiritual abuse in the literature. Dehan and Levi define spiritual abuse in the context of abused Haredi wives as "damaging the woman's spiritual life, spiritual self, or spiritual well-being, by means of purposely and repetitively criticizing, limiting, or forcing her to compromise or go against her spiritual conscience, resulting in a lowered spiritual self-image, guilt feelings, and/or disruption of transcendental connectedness" (2009: 1303). This is a narrow, highly specific characterization. David Ward's definition in contrast focuses on the misuse of power that is common in cases of spiritual abuse: "a misuse of power in a spiritual context whereby spiritual authority is distorted to the detriment of those under its leadership" (Ward 2011: 901). Finally, in developing their scale of spiritual harm and abuse, Daniel Koch and Leihua Edstrom define it as "a type of emotional and psychological abuse perpetrated by a religious leader or group and/or with a religious or spiritual component, usually involving coercion or control." Among the categories of spiritually abusive experiences they include pressure to maintain the religious system, embracing violence, controlling leadership, and gender discrimination, but there are arguments to be made for the addition of other categories such as spiritualized ableism, purity culture, and spiritualized racism (among others). Two aspects of these definitions are worth noting. First, on the first but not the latter two, persecution cases like *hijab*-snatching will not count as a kind of spiritual abuse, if the perpetrator is an outsider to the religious identity of the victim. Second, on Koch's and Edstrom's account, any spiritual component of abuse is at least conceptually separable from the other aspects. They say, "a survivor of clergy sexual abuse, then, is understood for our purposes to have been abused both sexually and spiritually. The sexual abuse can be expected to have effects on the survivor similar to other instances of sexual abuse, while the spiritual abuse will likely affect whether or how they are able to practice their faith" (477). Although I appreciate their emphasis on the uniquely spiritual impact of spiritual abuse, I am skeptical that aspects of the abuse are so easily separable, with the sexual aspects having the usual sexual impact and the spiritual aspects having a separate spiritual impact. I hypothesize, on the basis of years of engagement with religious trauma survivors, their narratives, and the small amounts of empirical data, that in "mixed cases" the abuse will have effects on the survivor that are distinct from other instances of the same kind of abuse in nonreligious contexts. Klaudia's story helps to illustrate this point. It is not just that she experiences her sexuality as dangerous or bad after the assault but that her negative perception of her sexuality is bound up with her perceptions of God, because God is the author of her sexuality, which she perceives as the cause of the priest abusing her. Thus, the spiritual and the sexual dimensions of trauma are deeply intertwined. If a therapist attempted to address only the sexual dimensions or only the spiritual ones, it seems likely that Claudia's pain would not be adequately understood.

There is also a great deal of overlap between religiously traumatic experiences and morally injurious ones. Spiritual abuse often involves betrayal by respected leaders who violate the moral and spiritual sensibilities of their followers. Community members may witness or become aware of abuse and feel unable to intervene. They may be pressured by religious leaders and teachings to engage in behaviors that violate their own conscience. They may develop a moral perspective at odds with some deeper sense of right and wrong. A gay evangelical may be morally injured by their decision to kiss someone of the same sex as themselves. A parent who violently "disciplines" their child because they have been told that God commands it may inflict religious trauma on their child and moral injury on themselves. While it is important to distinguish perpetrators from victims in individual instances, a single person can inflict or enable spiritual abuse while themselves being a victim of it. Consider a gay Christian who, despite the harm done to them, which they cannot acknowledge, encourages their fellow gay believers to undergo conversion therapy, or the woman who tries to "submit joyfully" to her husband's abuse while simultaneously denying that his abuse of their children is abuse at all. In both cases, an individual is experiencing spiritual abuse while also enabling it or inflicting it with respect to others. As such, in addition to healing from the trauma of their own experiences of abuse, they will need to address the guilt, shame, and distress of having harmed others or from having participated in becoming people morally distressed by witnessing others' perfectly acceptable behavior.

The second characteristic is that at least some of the post-traumatic effects have a religious object or trigger. Joel Hollier and his team report that "Nathan described how his heart began racing, and he became incredibly nervous as he stepped into a church for the first time in years. Katie spoke of her Complex [PTSD] flaring up each time she walks past a place of worship. Lisa shared that she would sit and cry on Sundays because people in her congregation had hurt her badly" (Hollier et al. 2022: 281). Others experience panic attacks and vomiting induced by exposure to certain religious music, religiously significant nightmares about the abuse, difficulty in prayer and other religious disciplines, among other things. One survivor says,

> Everything about church at the moment is triggering . . . it's hard to separate practices that are godly practices from the church that is institutionalized, unhappy, evilness . . . . So even singing worship in the car, even trying to pray, I get this instant pressure in my chest – that classic triggered feeling of "oh" uncomfortableness. It's like it doesn't feel right. I get this voice in my head saying, "God is not going to hear you" or "God is not going to engage with you." "You're in denial," and that kind of stuff. It's very hard to have an open and honest conversation with God when you don't fully believe in yourself that you are accepted by God because of the way you have been treated by the Church. (Hollier et al. 2022: 281)

Additionally, the moral emotions that often follow from trauma and moral injury may have religious realities, community, or even God as their object. Shame may be shame before God; anger may be at the Divine, at religious leaders, or religious communities; distrust may be of God, the self in relationship to God, and of those who worship God; guilt may feel like the judgment of God rather than a "mere" moral failure.

Third, the post-traumatic effects negatively impact the individual's ability to entertain or hold religious beliefs or engage in religious practices, or attitudes. In other words, someone is religiously traumatized when they have a religiously traumatic experience that inflicts lasting religious or spiritual harm. This is so in each of the case studies described earlier.

The removal of religious causation as a central feature of religious trauma may raise the worry that for some individuals, any trauma will count as a religious trauma, because all of life is interpreted through a religious frame of reference. I am unconvinced that this is a bad outcome. It is well-established in the literature that trauma of all kinds is spiritually significant (Pargament et al. 2005), and that positive and negative religious coping has a significant impact on outcomes following trauma (Smith 2004; Gerber et al. 2011). For a person who interprets any painful experience as divine retribution, any experience of a sexual assault might feel deeply religiously significant. Experiencing oneself as being punished by God through a sexual assault, especially if one cannot identify any failure that one judges deserving of such retribution, might result in religiously significant post-traumatic distress. One might feel betrayed by God. One might feel shame before God. Attempting to pray might trigger intrusive memories of the assault. I see no reason to exclude this case from the category of religious trauma.

There is no reason to worry that this entails that all trauma is religious trauma. Not everyone is religious, so not everyone will interpret experiences outside of religion as religiously significant, and not every religious person interprets every experience through a religious lens to the same degree as the person described earlier. Indeed, I suspect that such people represent a minority of religious individuals. So it is unlikely that all trauma will end up being a form of religious trauma. But even for those religious folks who interpret most of their life experience through a religious lens, there are still degrees of religious significance. Even for the person described earlier we can imagine that being assaulted by her priest would be more religiously traumatic than assault by a stranger or even a trusted person. Just as post-traumatic distress admits of degrees, we can assume that religious trauma does as well. Something may be extremely traumatic but only mildly religiously traumatic, while something that looks like a minor stressor might be extremely religiously traumatic because of its religious significance. For example, threat of rejection by close friends might be moderately traumatic for anyone, but the threat of shunning or rejection from a religious community might be deeply religiously traumatic because it represents being cut off from the divine or the community of God.

2.4 Spiritual Struggle and Spiritual Agency

As mentioned in the first section, it is difficult to draw general conclusions about the impact of trauma on agency, and even in individual cases we should exercise epistemic humility. Nonetheless, evidence about the impact of trauma on the body and mind explored in the first section gives us reason to think that, in some cases, some of the religiously significant impacts of spiritual abuse can undermine spiritual agency in ways that excuse them from religious or spiritual obligation.

Consider someone who experiences intrusive memories of sexual violation upon entering a church, mosque, or temple. This individual might experience any subset of the following symptoms: panic, disgust, shame, guilt, fear, rage, unwanted bodily responses such as sexual arousal, elevated heart rate, trembling, nausea, vomiting, disorientation, or dizziness. It is not difficult to imagine these responses rendering the individual unable to force themself over the threshold. Even if the person could get through the door, it is not unreasonable to think that the person who chose not to try to participate in religious practices, because the cost was too high, has a religious excuse (akin to moral excuse) for this choice, even if some religious practices are usually religiously obligatory. Failing to participate in such a case might be comparable to failing to participate while one is physically injured. Furthermore, it is unclear whether the individual who, out of love for or fear of God, pushes through these barriers to engaging in religious practices would thereby achieve something spiritually valuable. In many religious traditions merely going through the motions of spiritual practice does not satisfy one's spiritual obligations. Practitioners are supposed to love, worship, trust, and submit to God. While each of these may have behavioral implications, none (except possibly the last) is reducible to mere behavior. Some post-traumatic responses are at odds with these attitudinal and affective aspects of these religious obligations. It is difficult to trust a being before whom one feels deep shame, fear, guilt, or rage. It is doubtful that one can worship when one feels moral horror and disgust toward the required object of worship. If this is true, religious trauma survivors can be incapacitated or hindered with respect to both the practices and the attitudes of religious devotion as the result of factors outside of their immediate, conscious control.

In addition to undermining spiritual agency, religious trauma might render new religious choices and beliefs practically and epistemically rational for the survivor. It is often practically rational to avoid situations that one is justified in regarding as dangerous. Consider the story in the Tanakh [which Christians call the Old Testament] of Uzzah touching the ark of the covenant to steady it. God strikes Uzzah dead for his disrespect, and David, afraid of the risk posed by such a dangerous object, has the ark sent away. Setting aside Uzzah's and God's moral and religious justifications for their actions, David's response appears deeply practically rational. The ark is dangerous! Thus it is practically rational to form the intention to stay away from the ark. Similarly, there is something practically rational about the survivor of religious trauma forming the intention to stay away from the sources of physical, moral, and spiritual injury, whether that is a religious text, leader, practice, community, or religion as a whole. This might look like a choice to leave a particular church, no longer listening to the teaching of a certain rabbi, spending more time on secular concerns than religious ones, refusal to go to confession or any number of things. It might even involve complete disaffiliation from religion.

Insiders to the religious tradition may doubt whether such avoidant behaviors are what the survivor has an *ultima facie* reason to do. But it seems uncontroversial that past experience gives the survivor a *prima facie* reason, and a very strong one at that, to avoid such risks. And if it is a *prima facie* reason, it might end up being an *ultima facie* reason depending on other religious and personal details of the situation. An insider might also think that even if religious trauma gives survivors temporary reasons to cease engaging in certain religious practices and attitudes, the truth of the claims of the religious tradition also give the survivor strong reasons to try to recover from the impact of the trauma so that they may return. It may be true that if a religious tradition is true and good, it would be in the survivor's best interest not to be permanently alienated from it. However, it is important to remember that historically, clinical treatment for post-traumatic distress is a new development, and folk practices of soul care within various cultures vary from the deeply effective and healing to radically harmful. In the West, as recently as the beginning of WWI, post-traumatic distress was regarded as moral weakness and treated by dubious means, such as adversarial critique and electric shock therapy (Fassin and Rechtman 2009). Today, therapy is often expensive, not covered by insurance, in short supply in rural and marginalized communities, and not available all over the world. Treatment for post-traumatic distress has varying success rates, and evidence-based therapy for specifically religious trauma is still in its infancy. Community practices of mourning, bearing witness, testifying, and caring in the wake of traumatic suffering have and continue to exist in different forms in cultures the world over, but because these practices are often intertwined with the very religious traditions and practices that have caused harm, one cannot assume that tools for healing will be available to everyone who needs them. In other words, healing from religious trauma (whatever that amounts to) may be a valuable goal, but it is unlikely to be available to everyone, and even when it is available, healing is a slow, sometimes life-long, process without guaranteed results. As such, the philosophical and theological answer to "what about people who cannot trust God because of religious trauma?" should not depend primarily on the possibility of healing.

Finally, like trauma more generally, the effects of trauma on agency are not always uniformly bad. Survivors of religious trauma are currently among the fiercest voices for reform in each of the religious traditions mentioned in this section. People living with the effects of religious trauma are often able to see the connection between theology and abusive practice and between religious structures and practices on one hand and vulnerability to abuse and misuses of power one the other with a clarity that others lack. As we will briefly consider in the last section, the capacity for dissociation sometimes developed in trauma is correlated with some valuable spiritual skills and experience, such as the ability to enter trance states and success in meditation. Trauma survivors possess skills and wisdom that they have developed in the midst of horror that they and their communities may value. However, we must not regard these as silver linings to weigh in the scales of cosmic justice against the horror of the trauma. We must bear witness both to the horror of spiritual abuse and to the wisdom and agency of survivors if we are to do either justice.

3 The Social Epistemology of Religious Trauma

Religious trauma rarely occurs in a social vacuum, disconnected from religious community. Religious people typically believe, love, worship, and, yes, abuse in community. One common, irreducibly social dimension of religious trauma are the patterns of (un)knowing that create the conditions for, shape the experience of, and inform the response to spiritual abuse. This section explores three central aspects of the social epistemology (the area of philosophy having to do with knowledge) of religious trauma: (1) the ways in which religious concepts and discourse can prevent sufferers from understanding their experiences of religious trauma, and from communicating them to others, (2) how these concepts and discourses interact with power structures to ensure the ignorance of the community, and (3) how respect for the epistemic privilege of survivors might offer part of the epistemic path toward addressing religious trauma.

3.1 Not Knowing

Miranda Fricker defines hermeneutical injustice ("hermeneutics" has to do with interpretation of texts and discourse) as "the injustice of having some significant area of one's social experience obscured from collective understanding owing to a structural identity prejudice in the collective hermeneutical resource" (Fricker 2007: 155). By "hermeneutical resources," Fricker means something like socially available conceptual schemes, predominant understandings of the social world, and their semantic designations. By "structural identity prejudice," she refers to prejudices against individuals in virtue of their social identity that manifest not only in individual attitudes but in the very ways that societies are structured. Under unjust conditions, there are aspects of life where "the powerful have no interest in achieving a proper interpretation" (152). This can result, on the one hand, in members of the less powerful groups lacking the conceptual resources necessary to correctly understand and communicate significant aspects of their experience (hermeneutical injustice), or, on the other hand, in members of the more privileged group willfully refusing to learn or engage with the hermeneutical resources that marginalized communities have already developed. This is what Kristie Dotson calls contributory injustice (Dotson 2012) and Gaile Pohlhause calls willful hermeneutical ignorance (Pohlhaus 2012).

Consider, first, hermeneutical injustice. While Fricker herself often writes of hermeneutical injustice in terms of hermeneutical gaps (cases where a concept is completely missing from the hermeneutical repertoire), I have argued elsewhere that there are important cases where all of the relevant conceptual resources exist within the dominant community, but value-laden concepts encourage miscategorization of experiences. This miscategorization distorts understanding of one's own experiences and keeps one from knowing or understanding its moral contours (Panchuk 2020). Lani's theological framework encourages her to believe that it "was [her parents'] God-given duty to show love" by beating her (Harper 2013b). As a result, even though she has the concept of "abuse" and could recognize it in other contexts, her theological framework excludes her own suffering from this description. Aisha is told that the harassment she experienced – an experience she is able to recognize and name – is part of *haqiqa* rather than abuse. Her act of resistance in reporting harassment is re-interpreted as the sin of "backbiting a wali." As a result, she cannot initially understand the judgment and blame directed at her by members of her community as victim-blaming. This framework causes her to doubt her initial understanding and temporarily prevents her from fully grasping the nature of her own experience. We can think of these as first-order misclassifications because the victim categorizes their experience under the wrong action or experience-type: "discipline" instead of "abuse" in Lani's case and *haqiqa* instead of "harassment" in Aisha's case.

At the second-order level, an individual may understand their own experience as falling under the correct action-type, but, for similar reasons, understand those action-types as falling under the wrong higher-order type. Both Klaudia and Devorah know that they are being sexually assaulted, but rather than understanding assault as something for which they bear no guilt or shame before God, their theological frameworks (and perhaps general cultural narratives that blame victims) encourage them to understand the abuse as something they should have been able to stop, and something for which God must be angry – as their own sin.

In each of the earlier cases, the victim is harmed as a knower, because they cannot fully understand their experiences or explain them to others. They are harmed as agents, because their lack of knowledge prevents them from acting in accordance with their true interests and values. Together these result in social, personal, and religious harms. First, if one does not know that one is being abused, or that God would want one to be protected from abuse, then one is more likely to be subjected to the abuse for longer, which in turn may increase the likelihood and severity of any post-traumatic effects. Second, abusers often target and groom people who are unlikely to be able to recognize or escape the abuse. Thus, the same religious discourse that makes it difficult for some religious practitioners to recognize abuse may make them more vulnerable to being abused in the first place.

Finally, the skewed hermeneutical resources may themselves be spiritually traumatic. Consider the examples of spiritual abuse of LGBTQ+ evangelicals described in the last section. It is not only that believing that their sexuality is an abomination prevents LGBTQ+ Christians from recognizing practices of religious conversion therapy as abusive. The very internalization of the theological perspective is itself spiritually violent (Tobin 2016), causing LGBTQ+ Christians to perceive God as disgusted with and even fundamentally against them. Similarly, the possibility that a violation of sexual boundaries could be part of *ruqya* or *haqiqa* may be both traumatic and damaging to a Muslim's relationship to the Divine and the religious community, whether or not one is actually subjected to any form of sexual harassment. Lani struggles in her relationship with God even after escaping her abusive family. Not only can love, divine and human, never be a source of refuge, comfort, or safety within this theological framework, but even after a person has rejected the framework, the affective resonance of those concepts may linger, causing love to continue to feel unsafe or triggering.

There are no doubt numerous other social epistemic mechanisms that can serve to harm sufferers of religious trauma in their identity as knowers. Testimonial injustice, gaslighting, educational neglect, and outright lies, among others, can all serve to undermine knowledge in ways that are themselves religiously traumatic, keep the victim from understanding that they are experiencing abuse or violence, and make escape from the spiritual environment more difficult. I suspect that the practices of high control groups that have sometimes been called "brain washing" include a combination of just such epistemic practices. But what is crucial to keep in mind is that while "brain washing" has the connotations of a practice completely outside the control of the subject, the epistemic landscape described in this section, while hostile to knowledge and agency, does not fully undermine the subject's epistemic agency. Rather, it corrupts agency, rendering what it is most rational for the individual to believe, given their evidence, something deeply at odds not only with reality, but with their own goals and values. It is this corruption of epistemic and spiritual agency that is so insidious, because it renders victims complicit in their own victimization.

3.2 Needing Not to Know

Victims of religious abuse and trauma are not the only ones whose knowledge is limited by spiritually abusive systems. Enablers, communities, and even perpetrators themselves can also manage not to know about the abuse happening in their midst. As Judith Herman puts it,

> It is very tempting to take the side of the perpetrator. All the perpetrator asks is that the bystander do nothing. He appeals to the universal desire to see, hear, and speak not evil. The victim, on the contrary, asks the bystander to share the burden of pain. The victim demands action, engagement, and remembering ... The perpetrator's argument prove irresistible when the bystander faces them in isolation. Without a supportive social environment, the bystander usually succumbs to the temptation to look the other way. This is true even when the victim is an idealized and valued member of society ... When the victim is already devalued (a woman, a child), she may find that the

> most traumatic events of her life take place outside the realm of socially
> validated reality. Her experience becomes unspeakable. (Herman 2015: 7–8)

In explaining hermeneutical injustice, Fricker notes that there are aspects of life where "the powerful have no interest in achieving a proper interpretation" (152). They do not need to know and so do not care to name or learn names for these experiences. But in addition to not needing to know, sometimes humans need not to know. We can have an interest in not knowing truths that are uncomfortable or make moral demands on us. Linda Martín Alcoff calls this the difference between "ignorance [as a] feature of neglectful epistemic practice [and] as a substantive epistemic practice in itself" (Alcoff 2007: 39). Sometimes it is the individual who wants not to know things. These can be one-off cases of self-deception or willful ignorance, and can range in significance from merely silly (believing one's favorite underdog team will win the next world series against the evidence) to deeply pernicious (refusing to recognize that one's overuse of alcohol is harming others). But in addition to cases of individual intentional ignorance, communities of epistemic practice may be constructed to facilitate willful ignorance among those who benefit from not knowing. Mills gives the example of how the conceptual framework of "savage" and "civilized" made it possible for the framers of the constitution to write of the equality of all men while simultaneously dispossessing vast numbers of men of their land and counting others as three-fifths of a free person without any sense of cognitive dissonance. An entire way of life depended on these practices, and so there was deep motivation not to know that Black and Indigenous people are members of the moral community. This unknowing required a tailor-made conceptual framework and practices of avoidance that would keep the community from facing evidence to the contrary (Mills 2007: 26–27). Mills calls this "white ignorance." In philosophy, epistemologies of ignorance have given most attention to ignorance related to racial and gender-based oppression (Ortega 2006; Fricker 2007; Mills 2007; Dotson 2012; Medina 2012; Pohlhaus 2012), but they occur in religious contexts as well.

In the context of religious trauma, both those holding institutional power and the general community (especially those members least vulnerable to victimization) often need not to know of the reality and pervasiveness of abuse within their communities. Knowing might threaten a status quo in which they find comfort and meaning. This need can result in conceptual frameworks and epistemic practices aimed at maintaining ignorance. Sometimes leaders who do know about religious abuse simply lie and cover up the facts in order to prevent others from knowing. More insidious are practices that facilitate the unknowing of the leaders themselves. The very hermeneutical resources that encourage people like Lani and Aisha to misunderstand their own experience can allow their abusers and the community to convinced themselves that no one is being abused. It is fully possible that Lani's parents did not believe they were abusing their children and that the *Shaykh's* community did not believe he was sexually harassing women, because they were participating in and benefiting from epistemic systems that facilitate this unknowing. Abusers are culpable for their abuse, even when they don't fully recognize they are doing it, because they *should know* that what they are doing is wrong. Furthermore, we are responsible for self-deception and willful ignorance. Theological frameworks that sanctify harm may explain how abusers and enablers are able not to know, but it does not exonerate them.

Kristie Dotson describes a specific kind of willful ignorance especially relevant to religious trauma. This is contributory injustice (2012). Contributory injustice occurs when a marginalized community has developed the conceptual resources to make their experiences intelligible to themselves and to others, but the dominant community refuses to engage with or give sufficient up-take to those resources. As online survivor communities, documentaries, and social media discourse around spiritual abuse and religious trauma have exploded over the past decade, survivors are increasingly developing the hermeneutical resources to make their experiences intelligible. The very existence of terms such as "church hurt," "spiritual abuse," "spiritual violence," religious trauma," "spiritual bypassing," "sacramental shame," and "deconstruction" and social media movements such as "#churchtoo," "#mosquemetoo," "#GamAni" (Hebrew for "me too"), and "#shultoo" all demonstrate that survivors and their allies have come together to name and describe their experience.

Contributory injustice is what happens when religious communities refuse to take up, or willfully misinterpret, the significance of these conceptual resources. This can happen when a community refuses to engage with the resources at all, by continuing to treat those experiencing the impact of religious trauma as "in rebellion against God" for their failure to engage "appropriate" religious practices and attitudes. Alternatively, communities may acknowledge the existence of the hermeneutical resources, but deny that they accurately describe reality. One sees this when religious leaders say that the stories shared by #mosquemetoo are made up or exaggerated by people wanting to "backbite a wali," when they claim that "spiritual abuse" is a term made up by those who do not want to submit to "biblical discipline," that those who "deconstruct" just want to have promiscuous sex, or that talking about trauma proves the survivor is bitter. Finally, contributory injustice can manifest in the appropriation of these concepts for uses that undermine the goals for which they were developed. Consider, for example, the appropriation of the concept of "grooming" by those who oppose the exposure

of children to the existence of people with non-cisheteronormative gender identities and sexual orientations in the church. "Grooming" describes the process by
which an abuser targets, tests, and prepares a potential victim for the abuse.
It often involves displays of affection and care, small boundary violations, and
isolation, so that when the abuse begins the victim has little recourse. Calling it
"grooming" to allow queer Christians to exist openly in church serves to associate
queer Christians with child abusers, to vilify those who affirm them, and to
undermine attempts to deploy the concept of grooming to protect children from
real harm. Similarly, it is a form of contributory injustice when pastors call
demands for accountability for wrongdoing "spiritual abuse." All of these
practices help maintain ignorance, not only of those in positions of institutional
power, but also of the members of the community who need not to know about
religious trauma in order for their illusions about their faith not to be destabilized.
It is terrifying to face the possibility that (parts of) the community and practices
that one thought nourishing are actually rotten.

3.3 Knowing Religious Trauma

While epistemic environments that foster conditions for religious trauma can
occlude understanding for victims and their communities, being marginally
situated within a community because of religious abuse can impart epistemic
benefits. Standpoint epistemologists have long argued that one's social situation
shapes what one can and cannot know, and what one needs, does not need, and
needs not to know. As Pohlhaus notes, "repeated over time, [experiences of
oppression] can lead to habits of expectation, attention, and concern, thereby
contributing to what one is more or less likely to notice and pursue as an object
of knowledge in the experienced world" (2012: 717).

Consider the difference between an abusive parent and the abused child. The
abusive parent may not have an interest in, and perhaps a vested interest in not,
understanding how the abuse feels to the child. The child, on the other hand, has
a deep interest in understanding the moods, preferences, habits, and desires of
the abuser. They need to understand how the abuser sees the world in order to
placate the abuser as much as possible. The child may be forced to develop
a vision of the world as it seems to themselves and a vision of the world as it
seems to the abuser. Feminist epistemologists sometimes call this phenomenon
"double vision," borrowing from W. E. B. DuBois's concept of "double
consciousness." Thus, the standpoint epistemologist argues, the marginalized
may not just have knowledge of different things than the privileged. They may
have more complete and accurate knowledge in certain domains. Furthermore,
such a social position can encourage one to foster an awareness of the human

tendency to only see certain things. As José Medina puts it, "the realization of one's [social] invisibility entails that one becomes to oneself – painfully, sometimes even traumatically – the living proof that there is more to be seen than what others (some others) see" (2012: 191–192). He also notes that when responded to correctly, this realization can motivate the epistemic virtue of meta-lucidity – an awareness of "the effects of oppression on our cognitive structures and of the limitations in epistemic practices (of seeing, talking, hearing, reasoning etc.) grounded in relations of oppression" (192). Nothing about being socially marginalized guarantees meta-lucidity, and being socially privileged does not preclude it. Rather, Medina and most contemporary standpoint epistemologists speak of tendency and opportunities to achieve a particular epistemic stance afforded by social position. Furthermore, feminist epistemologists note that there are deep personal and epistemic costs to double vision and the epistemic labor that it requires (Narayan 2004).

Those who have experienced religious trauma are socially positioned as epistemically privileged with respect to spiritual abuse and religious trauma in their particular religious environment. This is the case, first, because religious trauma is a transformative experience. According to L. A. Paul, a transformative experience is one that transforms the individual in at least two ways (Paul 2014). First, it transforms them epistemically, giving them access to knowledge of what the experience is like. Second, it changes one's values, preferences, and goals.

The person who has experienced spiritual abuse and religious trauma may know what it is like to feel as if God's presence is woven into the very experience of abuse, to fear that God hates one's very capacity for loving others, or to have the melanin levels in one's skin referred to as a curse inflicted for murder. The survivor may also develop new values, preferences, practices, and goals that directly flow from their experience. Religious trauma survivors are often especially attentive to the warning signs of abuse and to religious structures that render people more vulnerable. They may place higher value on institutional transparency, on interpersonal care, and on bearing witness to the suffering of others. This collection of knowledge, epistemic virtues, and values can place them in a position of epistemic privilege with respect to religious trauma. This does not happen automatically. A religiously traumatized person may be deeply invested in not acknowledging their own victimization or the extent of its impact in their life. Nonetheless, the experience of trauma may be part of what places some survivors in a position to know and develop virtues that would be difficult to attain via other means.

When it comes to traumatic experience, people who have not experienced a particular kind of trauma tend not to be good at grasping what such

experiences are like or at recognizing the degree to which they do not understand what such experiences are like. The deep epistemic changes that are
a classic response to traumatic experiences point in this direction. How could
it be that exposure to horrors radically changes our understanding of the world,
and of ourselves, if most of us are already aware that sexual assault, child abuse,
war, and natural disasters are common human experiences, and if we already
understand what they are like? We know that they exist, and we know that they
are deeply bad. But they tend only to shake our faith or cause us to question our
assumptions about the justice and good in the world when we or someone we
love experiences them directly. This suggests that we did not previously fully
appreciate either what the experiences were like or our own ignorance of it.

One might chalk this up to a failure of empathy or to irrationality. In the
introduction to his book on theodicy, Peter van Inwagen suggests that it is "just
irrational" for a woman to begin doubting her faith when her own child is
diagnosed with cancer when she already knew that other people's children die
of cancer and that did not cause her to doubt the existence of a loving God (van
Inwagen 2006: 10). While van Inwagen rightly acknowledges that it would be
stupid and cruel to say such a thing to a grieving mother, I also think that it would
likely be false. A better explanation of these phenomena is that (1) there are some
experiences that we simply cannot correctly imagine or cognitively model until
we have had them, as per Paul's account of transformative experience, (2) our
epistemic practices discourage us from attending appropriately to the evidence
that we do not know what these experiences are like before we have had them, and
(3) our social world obscures the ways in which this ignorance shapes our
preferences and values. We are invested in not recognizing that our faith might
have been shaken if our lives had gone differently and that our favorite theodicy
might not assuage our doubts if we had suffered more or differently.

With respect to the lived experience of spiritual abuse and religious trauma,
the average religious individual appears to be like a version of Frank Jackson's
Mary (a color scientist who knows all of the relevant facts about color vision but
who has spent her entire life in a black and white room and has never experienced the color red for herself) who, prior to exiting her black and white room, is
confident that there is no significant difference between her understanding of
color vision and the painter's, and that her values and preferences will not be
significantly changed by whatever she experiences when she steps outside
(Jackson 1986). She does not know what seeing red is like and she does not
understand the sense in which she does not know what seeing red is like.
Moreover, she does not understand how this lack of knowledge shapes her
preferences and values. Not only does the average, religious individual who has
not experienced religious or spiritual abuse not know what religious trauma is

like, but religious institutions often make it difficult, via denial, deflection, or the vilification of survivors, to attend to the stories and experiences of survivors in a way that would help them recognize either their ignorance or the way their ignorance facilitates their comfort.

When we combine the potential epistemic privilege of survivors with the epistemic disadvantage and potential epistemic vices of the general community, we see why it behooves religious communities to listen attentively to the testimony of survivors, and to exercise toward them testimonial, hermeneutical, and contributory justice. Testimonial justice requires that the listener ratchet up their credibility judgments with respect to survivors, knowing that identity prejudice, as well as their lack of comprehension of the lived experience of religious trauma, may make them prone to inappropriately low credibility judgments (Fricker 2007: 90–91). Hermeneutical justice requires special effort to make sense of the testimony of those who may not have the full hermeneutical resources to make their experience and their judgments communicatively intelligible. It requires working creatively with the speaker to elucidate difficult to describe reality (Fricker 2007: 171–173). And finally, contributory justice would motivate the community to educate themselves in and adopt the hermeneutical resources offered by the religious trauma survivor community and their allies. These things are required for epistemic justice not because survivors are always right or because they always agree among themselves, but because they are positioned to have the knowledge and develop the epistemic character, values, and practices with respect to religious trauma that are lacking in the community at large. They can provide needed epistemic friction to the status quo that benefits the community epistemically and spiritually.

José Medina postulates that some marginalized people who have developed the "meta-lucidity" mentioned earlier find themselves in a position to radically challenge the epistemic norms of the society at large. These become "epistemic heroes," not because they necessarily do more than others to challenge the epistemic environment, but because, for a combination of reasons, their actions become well-known enough to become emblematic and echoable (repeatable) in ways that result in chained epistemic action (2012: 229). Medina presents Rosa Parks as an epistemic hero of the civil rights movement. For Medina, Parks's actions are not best understood in an individualistic way as a lone woman choosing in isolation to refuse to give up her seat, but in the context of a social movement in which it had become intelligible for her action to be seen as an act of resistance, emblematic of the practices of the entire movement, and repeatable by others in joint, chained actions (234–248).

With respect to religious trauma, the world has been blessed with many epistemic heroes, and individual religious communities also have their own who function as local epistemic heroes. Within Christianity, the survivors who, like Phil Saviano, spoke out against abuse in the Catholic Church and collaborated with journalists from *The Boston Globe* to shed light on a systemic cover-up of abuse, became epistemic heroes. Even though we do not know all of their names, we know the epistemic work that they did. As with Parks, their epistemic courage was made possible by a number of social factors, including the emergence of stories of Catholic clergy sexual abuse in Ireland, journalists who were willing to tell their stories, and a public that was ready to listen. A full decade before *The Boston Globe* went public with their stories, Sinéad O'Conner ripped up a picture of the Pope on *Saturday Night Live* in protest of clergy sexual abuse. She faced severe backlash for this choice, but wrote in an open letter about it that

> The only reason I ever opened my mouth to sing was so that I [could] tell my story and have it heard ... My story is the story of countless millions of children whose families and nations were torn apart in the name of Jesus Christ ... So, it has occurred to me that the only hope of recovery for my people is to look back into our history. Face some very difficult truths and some very frightening feelings. It must be acknowledged what was done to us so we can forgive and be free. If the truth remains hidden then the brutality under which I grew up will continue for thousands of Irish children. And I must by any means necessary WITHOUT the use of violence prevent that happening because I am a Christian. Child abuse is the highest manifestation of evil. It is the root and effect of every addiction. Its presence in a society shows that there is not contact with God. And God is truth to me. (Hochman 1992)

Hers and others' actions were part of creating a world where Saviano and others could exercise the epistemic courage they did. They became emblems of a movement against Catholic clergy sexual abuse that has been echoed in chained actions around the world. People like Rachel Denhollender, Christa Brown, Jill and Jess Duggar, Debrah Feldman, Malkie Schwartz, Danish Qasim, and Danya Shakfeh might all be thought to play this role in their respective communities. They are epistemic heroes not because they are flawless, always right, or have necessarily done more than others, but because what they have done has received the public recognition necessary to serve as models that others may follow. Religious communities would do well to listen so that they can begin to know, and so that victims and survivors among them can more fully know their own experiences.

4 The Problems of Evil and Divine Hiddenness

The problems of evil and divine hiddenness are two related but distinct families of argument from observations about the way the world is to the conclusion that the

God of classical theism does not exist. Apparently gratuitous suffering (suffering that does not seem to contribute to any greater good or to the prevention of any equal or worse evil) and God's apparent absence from our awareness and reflection seem, to many, to constitute strong evidence against the existence of an omniscient, omnipotent, and loving God. The connection between these two problems, both as philosophical objections to propositions about God's existence and as existential barriers to trust in God, can be seen especially vividly in Jewish theology in the wake of the Shoah. In much of that literature, the problem is not only that God allows the dehumanization and destruction of God's people, but that this permission manifests in God's apparent absence in the camps. Elie Wiesel writes of one of his fellow prisoners crying "Where is God?" as a young child is hung on the gallows on the night that "murdered [his] God and [his] soul" (Wiesel 2006: 34). In this moment, the problems of evil and divine hiddenness unite to constitute the lived experience of religious trauma. For Wiesel and others, the camps are not just sites of the trauma of torture, degradation, and death, but of the religious trauma of perceived abandonment by God.

Because the problems of evil and divine hiddenness have occupied a central place in contemporary philosophy of religion, it is worth considering how religious trauma might bear on our thinking about them. Perhaps most obviously, anyone who thinks that the purpose of human existence is to glorify God and enjoy God forever, or that union with God is the greatest good, should think religious trauma a very great evil given that it can undermine a person's capacity to fulfill the purpose of human existence and achieve the highest good. Religious trauma can obscure God's presence from people desperately seeking God. In other words, religious trauma is a striking instance of apparently gratuitous suffering and of the problem of divine hiddenness. As such, we can evaluate extant theodicies (attempts to respond to the problem of evil by positing the actual reasons God has for allowing suffering), defenses (responses that offer possible, but not necessarily actual, reasons God might have for allowing human suffering), and skeptical theistic responses (explained herein) with reference to religious trauma. This could be done in a number of ways. First, one might accept the boundaries of the current philosophical discourse and evaluate whether popular theodicies and defenses offer plausible, God-justifying reasons for allowing the spiritual suffering of, and apparent divine absence to, people in religious trauma. It might turn out that some theodicies and defenses could not explain religious trauma even if they are plausible with respect to other kinds of suffering. Second, one might ask how thinking about religious trauma challenges the discourse in a more fundamental way. One might ask if any extant theodicies or defenses themselves inflict or contribute to religious traumatization. Or, finally, following Amber Griffieon's work on "therapeutic theodicy" (which is not a theodicy at all in the standard sense of justifying the ways of God to man, but a *"reappropriation* of the term ... to signify ... the dynamic, diachronic, and irreducibly diverse struggle by which human beings wrestle with the problem of lived faith, the experience of suffering, and the witnessing to evil") we might ask what ways of thinking about and imagining the divine might be helpful in reconciling the life of faith with the realities of religiously traumatic suffering (2018: 4). Each of these approaches offers a valuable direction of philosophical inquiry, demanding more careful work than is possible in a book of this length. Nonetheless, in what follows, I sketch some brief examples of how each of these projects might take shape.

4.1 Evaluating Theodicies and Defenses in Light of Religious Trauma

A popular response to the problem of (moral) evil in contemporary philosophy of religion is the Free Will Defense, argued for most influentially by Alvin Plantinga, but also defended by post-holocaust theologians like Eliezer Berkovits. On this view, God does not directly cause the suffering and evil in our world. God simply creates human beings with free will and gives them the space to develop and exercise it. According to Plantinga, God cannot both create free beings and guarantee that they never use their freedom for evil (Plantinga 1989: 34–44). If free will is a great enough good, then God is justified in creating beings with it, even though doing so creates the possibility of evil and suffering. For Berkovits, God's apparent absence to believers in some suffering is a necessary condition for the full realization of human freedom. He says, "[t]hat man may be, God must absent himself" and that "[God's] very love for man necessitates the abandonment of some men to a fate that they may well experience as indifference to justice and human suffering" (Berkovits 1973: 107–109).

In her recent book *God, Suffering, and the Value of Free Will*, Laura Ekstrom challenges the notion that free will is a great enough good to justify the kinds and degrees of suffering caused by it (2021). Many, including Plantinga, assume without argument that free will is a very great good. But Ekstrom herself seriously doubts this. Religious trauma emphasizes some of her points in a particularly poignant way. If both free will and commitment to God are very great goods, then it is reasonable to think that freely loving, worshiping, and submitting to God is a great good. But religious trauma undermines some people's ability to freely choose to love and submit to God. As Melissa Raphael has argued in response to Berkovits, the free will defense entails that free will is such a great good that it is reasonable to sacrifice the human dignity and free will of some (those whose agency is undermined by abuse and suffering) so that others may freely exercise theirs (those who choose to abuse them) (Raphael 2004). For Raphael, Berkovits's account makes the degradation of women, children, and men "feminized by their powerlessness" the price of "masculine becoming" (Raphael 2004: 136). In the context of religious trauma, it seems that the very great good of some people's religious and spiritual agency is sacrificed for the "good" of some people being able to freely choose to abuse them.

Such considerations are not conclusive arguments against the free will defense. The defender might insist that as long as the number of people who get to exercise free will in relationship to God outweighs the number of people whose free will is undermined, then God might still have a morally sufficient reason for allowing the suffering associated with loss of the religious and spiritual agency. Alternatively, one might think that those whose spiritual agency is so thoroughly undermined by religious trauma that they cannot engage in relationship with God are like anyone whose disability undermines their capacity for spiritual agency or interpersonal connection. If this is right, then religious trauma might be thought to constitute no more (or less) of a defeater for the defense than other kinds of disability. I think it is right to consider post-traumatic distress under the rubric of disability, and I am strongly committed to the view that, all other things being equal, people whose capacities for morally and spiritually responsible agency are limited or nonexistent due to disability can have lives worth living. However, responding to the problem posed by religious trauma by pointing out the goodness of lives where agency is significantly diminished is unlikely to be a promising approach for the proponent of the free will defense.

Others have thought that it is not enough for one person's suffering to be outweighed by a good experienced by someone else. Eleonore Stump, for example, develops a Thomistic response to the problem of suffering. She argues that, for Aquinas, the deepest desire of the human heart and the greatest good for humans is union with God. Flourishing as a human is distinct both from flourishing in mind and in body, because flourishing as a human involves obtaining the highest good and the deepest desire of the human heart. As such, suffering, even great suffering, can be compatible with human flourishing if it promotes the highest good. Furthermore, she argues that it is possible that whatever suffering God allows each person to experience is the best available means to bring about the greatest good for that person: to bring her into (greater) union with God. "Suffering," says Stump "is a means to human flourishing either because it is medicinal for those things disturbed in the psyche of a human person that keep him from being willing to let God be close to him, or because it is healing and instrumental in bringing a human person to greater closeness to God, or both" (2010: 457).

Similarly, a traditional view in Islam is that human suffering is not a theoretical problem to be solved, but a necessary aspect of human spiritual development

(Rouzati 2018). This is illustrated by a famous passage from the Sufi poet Rūmī's Mathnawī, which tells of a chickpea crying out to the woman cooking it in a pot, begging for relief from its suffering. The cook responds by saying, "I do not boil you because you are hateful to me; nay, 'tis that you may get taste; this affliction of yours is not on account of you being despised. Continue, O chickpea, to boil in tribulation, that neither existence nor self may remain to Thee" (Rouzati 2018: 10). This last bit of the line refers to the Sufi understanding of annihilation in *tawhid* – union with God so complete that the self ceases to exist as a distinct entity. The final end of suffering is union with God.

There is much to commend about Stump's and Rūmī's view. If anything can justify God's allowing the horrendous suffering of human persons, those sufferings being the best available means to give a person the greatest good and the deepest desires of their heart – union with God or *tawhid* – would be a strong candidate. It is also true that some kinds and degrees of suffering make us better people. No one develops virtues like courage, tenacity, and resilience without facing adversity. The question is, even if it is not logically impossible for the aforementioned accounts to obtain (there are no inconsistencies in the propositions), is it plausible to think that suffering of the kinds and degrees seen in the actual world tends to produce these outcomes when responded to correctly by the humans who experience them?

We know from the first section that traumatic suffering tends to have a disintegrating impact on the self, undermining agency and the capacity for interpersonal relationship. I argue elsewhere that the nature of traumatic suffering in general undermines the plausibility of Stump's defense (Panchuk 2023), but the evidence from religious trauma is particularly poignant. If the deepest desire of the human heart and what is truly best for us is union with God, and religious trauma does, in fact, undermine our capacity for engaging in relationship with God and in the religious and spiritual practices that facilitate that relationship, then it looks deeply implausible that religious trauma could be God's best means to give someone what is truly best for them or that it is something that could facilitate the achievement of *tawhid*. Of course, both Stump and the Sufi tradition affirm that human persons are imperfect. We do not always think, act, desire, and intend as we should. After briefly acknowledging the possibility of a "negative re-organization of the self" in the wake of suffering, Stump points out that just because any suffering that God allows has the power to be medicinal or healing, this alone cannot guarantee that the suffering will actually bring about the avoidance of the worst thing or the achievement of the best thing the human person can experience, because they can choose to exercise their free will otherwise (459). Thus, on Stump's view, those who do not spiritually benefit from their experience of religious trauma are personally responsible for this failure.

Such a response to apparent counter-evidence seems to defend the ways of God to man at the expense of (unintentional) victim-blaming and gaslighting. The view not only entails that victims are at fault for not benefiting from their suffering, but may make them doubt the veracity of their own experience of the trauma and its aftermath as something they could not have chosen to spiritually benefit from. Of course, no survivor can prove that they have not chosen not to heal and be reconciled to God. Nor can they prove with certainty, while they are alive to do so, that the religious trauma will not have spiritually benefited them by the end of their life. But to insist on believing that they have, or that it will, in the face of their testimony to the contrary and in the absence of very strong evidence, simply because it would vindicate God, seems cruel and unloving. Such claims may compound the guilt and shame of existing religious trauma or even constitute a new instance of it. Little is more traumatic than to face unspeakable abuse in the name of God only to be told that one's own account of the impact of that abuse is untrustworthy because it conflicts with the community's theology.

Another theodicy that may perpetuate religious trauma is the divine intimacy theodicy. Michael Harris, for example, draws on Rabbinic teachings to argue that the concept of *yissurin shel ahavah*, "the afflictions of love," is best understood not as a punishment theodicy or as a soul-making theodicy, but as a species of divine intimacy theodicy. According to Harris, intimacy with the divine may be experienced not only through suffering, where God is present to the individual as they suffer, but in suffering. When intimacy is experienced *in* suffering, (1) God directly causes the suffering, and (2) the very act of inflicting the suffering is an expression of divine love. God's is a "crushing, loving embrace," like a friend's whose hug is so tight that it hurts (Harris 2016: 81). However, God only visits such suffering on those who accept the suffering with love (82). In a footnote, Harris cites the Schottenstein translation of the Talmud as saying that *yissurin shel ahavah* "are visited upon a person only if they are accepted with consent" (82).[3]

It is important to note that Harris is neither trying to give a complete theodicy nor does he actually endorse *yissurin shel ahavah* as theodicy. He only claims that the concept should be understood in a certain way and that it might explain some instances of suffering. However, the picture of God inherent in such an account seems problematic. It paints God in the image of a human abuser. In truth, we only feel loved by the friend's overly tight hug if it does not actually harm us and if we know the friend is not intentionally hurting us. As soon as the discomfort turns to harm or is intentionally inflicted, the embrace ceases to be an

---

[3] I thank Samuel Lebens for pushing me to emphasize the significance of consent on Harris's account.

expression of love and becomes an act of abuse. If such a person were to declare, "I only hurt you because I love you," we would rightly condemn them as an abuser. One might think that the requirement for consent removes this concern. However, it is unclear whether in the context of the general Jewish ideal "of accepting divinely-imposed suffering with love and joy, or at least without complaint" (82), the belief that rejecting the suffering necessarily involves a rejection of the rewards of suffering (87), not to mentioned the infinite power differential between God and humans, that such consent could be sufficiently robust. Full-throated consent is undermined in a context where submission and consent are idealized in relationship to God and where refusal amounts to a refusal of intimacy.

Harris does not write about scenarios of religious trauma, so I cannot say if he would consider them candidates for instances of the afflictions of love. However, encouraging people of faith to perceive certain instances of suffering as having been caused directly by God, not as punishment, but as a pure expression of love, could itself be a source of religious trauma, particularly for people who have experienced abuse at the hands of human abusers who described the abuse in similar ways. Additionally, in suggesting that inflicting suffering is a legitimate way of fostering intimacy, Harris's theodicy may unintentionally render those who embrace it more vulnerable to and less likely to escape abuse coming from humans who claim to love them.[4]

4.2 Evaluating Skeptical Theism in Light of Religious Trauma

Skeptical Theism is a different kind of response to the problem of suffering. According to the skeptical theist even if an omniscient, omnipotent, omnibene-volent God has morally justifying reasons for allowing horrific suffering, finite beings like us should not expect to have epistemic access to those reasons. When presented with an atheistic argument from suffering, the skeptical theist will say that humans are not in a position to infer from their inability to see or imagine a reason that would justify God in allowing suffering that there is no such reason. Michael Bergmann suggests that skeptical theism is committed to the following skeptical theses:

(SC1) We have no good reason for thinking that the possible goods we know of are representative of the possible goods there are.

(SC2) We have no good reason for thinking that the possible evils we know of are representative of the possible evils there are.

---

[4] It is worth noting that even in the context of BDSM, *suffering* is not inflicted on the submissive partner. Mutual sexual *pleasure* is the aim, even when physical pain is involved.

(SC3) We have no good reason for thinking that the entailment relations we know of between possible goods and the permission of possible evils are representative of the entailment relations there are between possible goods and the permission of possible evils.

(3C4) We have no good reason for thinking that the total moral value or disvalue we perceive in certain complex states of affairs accurately reflects the total moral value or disvalue they really have. (Bergmann 2011: 379–382, 379)

If these accurately characterize the limits of human knowledge and the sort of epistemic humility that we should have with respect to the realm of value and to God, then, says the skeptical theist, we cannot make the atheistic inference. Michael Rea characterizes the central thesis of skeptical theism as the claim that:

(ST) No human being is justified (or warranted, or reasonable) in thinking the following about any evil e that has ever occurred: there is (or is probably) no reason that could justify God in permitting e. (Rea 2013: 483)

Although skeptical theism has primarily been used as a response to the problem of suffering, Michael Rea also offers a version of a skeptical response to the problem of divine hiddenness (2018). According to Rea, the problem of divine hiddenness is primarily a problem of violated expectations. Just as we expect good human parents to be present and available for relationship with their kids if they can, so too we expect God, as a perfect heavenly parent, to be present and available for relationship with us. Rea thinks that our human expectations are unjustified, particularly in light of the Christian doctrine of divine transcendence. According to Rea, we should not expect divine love to be similar to perfect human love, only ideal and unlimited, because humans are neither the proper object of, nor capable of enduring, unlimited union with the divine. So while it might be a form of neglect for human parents to be apparently absent, it cannot be rationally inferred that God's apparent absence is a sign of neglect or nonexistence.

The skeptical response may feel deeply familiar to survivors whose abusers told them that they were too immature, bad, or stupid to understand why the abuse was justified: "Just because you think you are being abused doesn't mean you are." "You may not understand now, but trust me. One day you'll understand that this is for your own good." "God says to do this, and God's ways are higher than your ways." Skeptical Theists claim that our ignorance of possible goods and evils and their entailment relations render us unwarranted in making the judgment that God lacks good reasons. Human abusers sometimes claim that a child's ignorance of possible goods and evils render them unwarranted in making the judgment that their abuser, and often God through the abuser, lacks justification for their behavior. But abused children sometimes *do* know that they are being abused, despite having reasons to accept that there is a moral knowledge gap between them and their abuser. Moreover, only their abusers, and those who may benefit from their abuse, wish them to accept that they are unwarranted in forming this belief. For a survivor who has had to work to overcome the epistemic injustice of being deprived of knowledge of their own abuse in this particular way, skeptical theism may suggest that their former self-doubt was not an injustice at all, but an appropriate manifestation of epistemic humility.

Even if the skeptical theist rejects a strong analogy between the two cases (the knowledge gap is greater in the divine case), it is still worth considering the moral significance of the resonance here. Should encouraging people to form true beliefs about God's reasons really involve making such similar arguments to those commonly made by abusers? The skeptical theist might respond that there are all sorts of things that are abusive when humans do them that are perfectly legitimate for God to do (e.g., requesting worship). But this misses the force of the objection. In both the divine and the human case, the central theses are *reasonable*. Humans have no good reason to think that all the goods they know of are representative of all the goods there are. A child has no good reason to think that all the goods they know of are representative of all the goods there are and about which their abuser knows, even if the child is in fact more morally perceptive in many senses than their abuser. The issue here is the way that genuine ignorance and reasonable epistemic humility are deployed to undercut warrant for taking oneself as a competent interpreter of one's own experiences of suffering.

Rea's skeptical response to the problem of divine hiddenness avoids this particular problem. Humans are not transcendent, and so we can evaluate human love according to the standard norms even though the concept cannot be applied literally to God. For Rea, a central question, then, is what makes it apt to apply the term "love" to God, when the concept diverges so greatly, when applied to God, from its sense when applied to humans. Rea sensitively answers this question in reference to those whose relationships with God are marred by religious abuse. One way the Christian God shows love to such people is by authorizing not only lament, but also protest directed toward God (a tradition of protest toward God is also prominent within Judaism). Rea writes,

> Often enough, lament and protest will remain accessible ways of continuing one's relationship with God and deliberately or not, promoting its improvement. They are behaviors that one can engage in just by trying to do so, assuming one has the concept of God, regardless of the state of one's confidence in God's existence, character, or dispositions toward oneself. They are,

furthermore, ways of drawing near to God despite one's own pain and despite the conflict that mars one's relationship with God. They are alternatives to abject submission to suffering, silence, and an unintelligible divine value scheme. (2018: 154)

Following Walter Brueggamnn, he further notes that relating to the divine in the mode of protest may help to strengthen the survivor's sense of self and personal agency following trauma. In a similar vein, Marilyn McCord Adams endorses "praying angry":

Praying angry helps to heal, because – by calling God to account – it asserts worth … Praying angry is an act of integrity: it foregoes politeness to tell stark truths about how the situation looked and felt to the survivor … it differentiates the survivor from God, from the Church, and from predator priests by daring to contradict official points of view. (2013)

I cannot overstate my appreciation for Rea's and Adams's work on this topic. Lament and protest in personal and corporate prayer are powerful and therapeutic tools for survivors and their communities to bear witness to suffering and to doing healing work (Panchuk 2023), and so I see Rea's contribution as in the spirit of Griffieon's call for therapeutic theodicy.

However, given a strong tradition in Christianity of modeling human love on the image of divine love, I fear that viewing God's apparent absence to those abused in the divine name as compatible with divine love may be harmful both to survivors and to religious communities. If God can love us while remaining silent and failing to intervene while we are being abused in God's name, and humans are to love as God loves, then those who, for their own comfort and ease, fail to protect the vulnerable, follow a divine example. It may be difficult for survivors to accept that those who failed to intervene on their behalf at little cost to themselves were failing to love them as they should, but that God's very same refusal is not evidence of the same failure of love. Of course, the philosopher can give myriad reasons why the reasons and obligations humans have differ from those God has. God may be justified in inaction while humans are not. But this approach, along with Rea's, challenges the popular idea that we should be "imitators of God." When humans imitate God, they may behave as moral monsters. The degree to which this is revisionary at the level of popular Christian thought, even if not in theological discourse, must be acknowledged and addressed.

5 Experiencing God, Traumatically

Religious experience is typically understood as an experience that seems to the subject to be of some external reality that has religious significance. Such experiences might be as mundane as a sense that one is loved by God or as mystical as union with the universe so profound that one's sense of self is dissolved. Over the past fifty years, work on religious experience in philosophy of religion has overwhelmingly focused on positively-valanced experiences of God and on the epistemic value of those experiences. Theists have argued that perception of God is not necessarily any more epistemically problematic than ordinary sensory experience (Alston 2014), that beliefs about God based on something like perception can be epistemically warranted (Plantinga 2000), or that religious experiences can constitute evidence for the existence of God (Swinburne 2004), either for the individual who experiences it or as part of a general cumulative case for Christianity. More recently, the conversation has expanded to explore the non-doxastic significance of religious experience (Griffioen 2016, 2021) and embodied, mediated experiences of God (Van Dyke 2018; Cockayne 2019). This section argues that thinking about religious trauma as a kind of religious experience can shed light on the phenomenon of religious experience and may also offer a potentially therapeutic (to some survivors of religious trauma) theodicy (Griffioen 2018).

5.1 Religious Trauma as Religious Experience

If religious experience is understood in the broadest possible sense as any experience of religion, then, of course, all religious trauma will count as a sort of religious experience, almost by definition. On the aforementioned narrower definition, a smaller but still very large proportion of religious trauma will count as religious experience, as it often involves experiences (as) of priests, religious practices, rituals, spiritual beings, and divine beings. Klaudia's story in section two illustrates a putative experience of God in line with Alston or Plantinga's perceptual models. Klaudia has an experience as of divine presence to her while being sexually abused by her priest. However, unlike most of the examples in contemporary philosophy of religion, she experiences God's presence as judgmental and cold. Some Jewish scholars have interpreted the holocaust as an experience of God's abuse of the people. Most notably, David Blumenthal argues that God's absence in Auschwitz is the absence of a complicit parent who is themself culpable for the abuse. "God is abusive, but not always... in this [abusive] mode, God "caused" the holocaust, or allowed it to happen" (1993: 247). In a similar vein, Former Hasidic Jew Deborah Feldman recalls her grandmother, a survivor of Borgen-Belsen, saying, in response to the new mandate from their rabbi that women shave their heads in addition to wearing wigs and headscarves, "Zeidy tells me that the rebbe wants us to be more ehrlich, more devout, than any Jew ever was. He says that if we go to extreme lengths to make God proud of us, he'll never hurt us again, like he did in the war" (Feldman 2012: 25). Blumenthal and Feldman's grandmother both express a desire to remain in relationship with and to please this abusive God, but also experience some level of distrust. Indeed, Blumenthal endorses protest against God's permissive abuse in the tradition of the prophets. Others, including child abuse survivor Diane, and feminist theologian Wendy Farley, have argued in correspondence with Blumenthal that if these experiences of God as abuser are indeed veridical, then neither the Jewish people nor anyone else should continue to worship and remain in covenant relationship with God. Diane says, "God, omnipotent and uncaring, is someone whom I would never wish to encounter again. I would stay as far away from Him as possible, forever. He would not be deserving of my company, comfort, praise, and love. Furthermore, I could not force myself to give anything to Him because fear, once felt can never be forgotten (Blumenthal 1993: 205–206).

Other experiences of God in religious trauma seem to be mediated by other spiritual realities that the individual experiences as an embodied being. When someone experiences awe as they gaze on a mountain vista, their religious experience is occasioned by their sensory experience of the view. Other times, religious experience is mediated in an even more profound way, as when the scent of frankincense in liturgy is experienced as smelling God, or the taste of wine on one's tongue is the taste of the Divine. Still other religiously traumatic experiences may be absence experiences, as the post-holocaust theology mentioned in the previous section suggests. And finally, religiously traumatic religious experiences may be of some other religiously significant reality that the individual closely associates with God. Nivedhan Singh describes the physical abuse that he experienced as a child at the hands of his father, an Episcopal Bishop, saying, "when I was a child, Bishop Singh was more than my father: he was my priest. When he beat me, God was beating me" (Singh 2023). Similarly, clergy sexual abuse survivor Barbara Blaine says of herself and other survivors, "Many of us feel as if we had been raped by God" (Doyle 2009: 247).

Just as one might experience the priest offering the host in the Eucharist as a mediated experience of Christ offering himself to the church, so Singh's experience of God beating him is mediated by his experience of his father beating him, as a priest. Lori, in contrast, does not experience her father's beatings as performed by God, but as performed at God's behest. Thus, for Lori, all other religious experiences will likely be mediated by her hermeneutical framework in which God is the kind of being who commands beatings. Consider the employee who is told by their immediate supervisor that the boss has told the supervisor to reprimand them for some minor infraction. Even though the employee does not have a direct perceptual experience of the boss, subsequent interactions with the boss will be mediated by the employee's understanding of the boss as unreasonably demanding. Similarly, Lori's belief that physical abuse is commanded by God will serve as part of the background from which she experiences God and other aspects of Christianity in the future. That is, the initial experience of abuse may be a negatively-valenced religious experience, but it may also shape the way Lori experiences God in all sorts of contexts in the future. Similarly, Aisha experiences the sexual harassment as sexual harassment by a *wali*, and at least temporarily as part of *ruqya*. Such an experience may shape her future experiences of both.

Finally, some kinds of religious trauma are experiences of other religiously significant realities. Consider the Haredi women who are abused by their husbands, the indigenous American children, and the LGBTQ+ evangelicals from section two. While there certainly may be some aspects of their experiences that are experiences of God, to a large degree the traumatic experience is religiously significant because of how it causes them to experience the self as a spiritual or religious being. The Haredi husband forces his wife to perform a violation of the religious law. The indigenous child is convinced that the Christian God views him as dirty. The LGBTQ+ Christian experiences their sexual urges as disordered or as abominations. Insofar as the human being is created by God and, in the three religious traditions considered in this volume, a being who is to live in relation to God, an experience of one's self as a spiritual being is itself an experience of a religiously significant reality – that is, a religious experience.

That there is a "dark side" of religious experience is fairly uncontroversial, even if not widely discussed in the philosophical literature. William James acknowledges as much in his classic work *The Varieties of Religious Experience* when he points out that religious mysticism is only half of mysticism. The other "lower" half he describes in terms of mental illness, while acknowledging their deep similarities to the religious kind (James 1902). While mental illness may cause negatively-valenced religious experiences, even deeply religiously traumatic ones, mental illness is not the primary locus of the kinds of religious trauma we have explored in this volume, nor are all the kinds of religious experiences prompted by religious trauma pathological.

The content explored in this volume is heavy and troubling. The effects of religious trauma reach the very core of the self and the very source of meaning and life. No words are adequate for such harm. Nonetheless, for many who have experienced religious trauma, the trauma itself has not had the last word. Survivors have found ways to exercise agency, free themselves, and rebuild new belief systems within or without religion in its aftermath. No doubt the paths forward will be as diverse as the survivors forging these paths. Nonetheless, in this final section, I suggest, however tentatively, two potentially agency-enhancing ways of thinking about religious trauma as religious experience: the connection between dissociation and mystical experiences and a therapeutic theodicy.

5.2 Dissociation and Mystical Experience

Recently, work in psychology and sociology suggests future directions for research into a connection between religious trauma and religious experience: the relationship between experiences of dissociation and the trait of absorption. Absorption is a personality trait described by psychologists as a "tendency to become deeply engrossed in sensory or imaginative experiences" (Lifshitz et al. 2019: 2) or "the capacity to become absorbed in inner sensory stimuli and to lose some awareness of external sensory stimuli" (Luhrmann 2005: 142). Dissociation, in contrast, is described by the American Psychological Association as a disintegration of integration of memory, perceptions, identity, emotions, and behaviors with one's sense of self, and is strongly associated with experiences of trauma. Classic symptoms of dissociation are amnesia, depersonalization, and derealization. Yet, absorption has been found not only to correlate strongly with the tendency to have religious experiences, from a more mundane sense of the presence of God in daily prayer to the likelihood of having intense and spiritually meaningful trips while on psychedelics (Luhrmann 2004; Luhrmann 2005; Lifshitz et al. 2019), but also with measures of dissociation (Luhrmann 2004; Luhrmann 2005; Lifshitz et al. 2019). While the explanation and significance of the overlap between absorption and dissociation remains highly controversial (Lifshitz et al. 2019), a number of studies have been done that are significant in considering the relationship between religious trauma and mystical and religious experiences.

In two provocative articles, Tanya Luhrmann argues that the frequency and character of dissociative symptoms in the wake of trauma that were common at both the beginning and the end of the twentieth century, but which all but disappeared in the intervening period, emerged from an interplay between the effects of trauma and the valorization of absorption and trance-like practices in American religious culture. That is, according to Luhrmann, people are more likely to respond to trauma in a dissociative way when non-pathological dissociative experiences, such as highly absorbing prayer, hearing God's voice, and or sensing God's presence, are normalized and celebrated within one's culture.

Others draw further connections between dissociation in trauma and in religious experiences. Some suggest that survivors of childhood trauma are more likely to become priests and priestesses in spirit-possession religions, although not all priests and priestesses have experienced trauma (Suryani & Jensen 1993; Castillo 1994; Chapin 2003, cited in Luhrmann 2004: 103), some studies find a correlation between past experiences of abuse and neglect and tendency to have religious or mystical experiences in one's religious practice (Kennedy and Drebing 2002; Parra 2019), although other studies have not found the same correlations or have found mixed results, depending on type of abuse (See for example, Kroll et al. 1996; Allen et al. 2002), and one study of Iranian college students found that, after recent trauma, previous religious abuse at any point in one's life was the strongest predictor of dissociative experiences (Nobakht and Yngvar Dale 2018). Moreover, Yochai Ataria shows that there is a deep experiential and conceptual overlap between traumatic experience and both mystical experiences and mindfulness practice. By presenting the first personal descriptions of both those who have had mystical experiences and those who have survived trauma, Ataria argues that both mystical and traumatic experience share the paradigmatic qualities associated with mystical experience: ineffability, noetic quality, transiency, passivity, unity, timelessness, and loss of sense of self. The trauma survivor writes:

> I feel like I was in hell. It was so dreadful that I lost understanding and feeling everything seemed dark. It was unreal dark all over. I know I am going to die. (Wilson 2006: 176, qtd in Ataria 2016: 338)

While the mystic reports:

> I seemed at first in a state of utter blankness [. . .] with a keen vision of what was going on in the room around me, but no sensation of touch. I thought that I was near death. (James 1902: 378, qtd in Ataria 2016: 338)

> I knew then that in the depth of my mind nothing was left that stood erect. This moment was a frightful one. [. . .] The days which followed this discovery were the saddest of my life. (James 1902: 175, qtd in Ataria 2016: 338)

Such research is inconclusive but deeply suggestive. Further research would be needed to say anything with confidence, but it is worth investigating whether the occurrence of trauma in a context where absorption has been cultivated by spiritual practices, and perhaps even trauma in moments of absorptive spiritual practice, as in many cases of religious trauma, may be part of explaining why spiritual abuse and other forms of religious trauma are so deeply spiritually impactful for the victim. Positive religious and mystical experiences tend to have a deep emotional and epistemic impact on the individual who has them. This is emphasized by recent research on the potential for psychedelics, which tend to produce mystical or transcendent experience, to reduce anxiety after terminal diagnoses, as treatment for PTSD, major depression, and obsessive-compulsive disorders (Pollan 2019). It is unsurprising that dissociation in traumatic experience, the neurobiological and psychological foundations of which are similar to mystical experience, would have a similarly global impact on one's beliefs and emotions. Moreover, myriad conversations with, and narratives from, religious trauma survivors provide anecdotal evidence that many survivors of religious trauma enjoyed a rich spiritual awareness and low-level religious experiences while in the abusive spiritual environment. Many took the burden of abuse to God in prayer; sought comfort in nature, or in spiritual practices such as singing hymns and songs of praise, receiving the Eucharist, or speaking in tongues; felt comfort or a sense of God's love and presence; heard God's voice; or sensed the leading of God. Others experienced a sense of God's judgment, conviction for spiritual or moral failings, or condemnation. Some experienced a confusing mixture of both. In either case, they were not strangers to religious experience. But there is, similarly anecdotal, evidence that the process of healing from trauma, which often involves the reduction of dissociative states and symptoms, also sometimes coincides with a reduction in the subjective sense of God's presence and care (as well as judgment and anger). This loss of a sense of God's presence sometimes leads to a feeling that one has been abandoned by God upon escaping abuse, as proof that the abusive community is right in their condemnation of outsiders. Alternatively, it can be experienced as a normal part of a deconversion process (i.e., once one stops believing in God, one stops experiencing the world as if God is in it). However, the opposite is sometimes true. Anecdotally, many religious trauma survivors have left spiritually abusive environments and found comfort and healing in spiritual practices more focused on mystical experience and other altered states of consciousness, such as druidry, Wicca, Buddhism, Norse paganism, various ancestral traditions of land-based spirituality, and other forms of New Age spirituality. Indeed, some view the ability to dissociate learned in trauma as a skill taken with them into their future spiritual practice. Further research would be needed to say anything scientific about such claims, but it is coherent with the account provided in the first section that trauma sometimes imparts skills and enhances aspects of agency.

5.3 Therapeutic Theodicy

Prior to her deconversion and subsequent rejection of the view, Laura Ekstrom argued that in addition to experiences of a putative objective reality that has religious significance, we might also include in the category of religious experience those experiences that "are of the same sort as experiences of a divine agent" (Ekstrom 2014: 269). This provided the foundation for her version of a divine intimacy theodicy. According to Ekstrom, when one suffers, one simultaneously undergoes a religious experience because one is undergoing an experience of the same sort as Jesus does at the cross. This similarity provides the grounds for a certain kind of intimacy. For Ekstrom, God allows us to suffer "in part because (i) this enables us to share in experience of God himself, where within the Christian tradition the focus is on appreciating deeply the passion of Christ; and (ii) this enables us vividly to experience the loving presence of God" (Ekstrom 2014: 272).

As a theodicy, I find her account unpersuasive. One's child need not experience religious trauma to experience intimacy with a religiously traumatized parent. Indeed, a good parent would pray that their child's faith be unmarred by such pain. To wish otherwise is nothing more than abject cruelty. Like Harris's, Ekstrom's view strikes me as painting an abusive picture of God. However, that need not discredit her insight that experiences *of the same kind* as a divine agent constitute a kind of religious experience. Indeed, a rich tradition exists of finding deep comfort in such resonances of experience. Black Liberation theologian James Cone finds meaning and hope in the face of Black suffering under white supremacy by drawing connections between the cross and of the lynching tree (2011). Jürgen Moltmann offers comfort after Auschwitz by presenting the image of the crucified God (1993). Even if the resonance between human and divine suffering is a poor theodicy, in the traditional sense of epistemically justifying the ways of God to man, it might still constitute a theodicy in Griffioen's sense of providing a way of imagining God that provides solace to those in the midst of suffering from religious trauma. In what follows, I argue that those who experience religious trauma, particularly in the form of spiritual abuse, experience something like what, according to the Christian and Jewish traditions, a divine agent experienced, and in Islam, a spiritually significant role model experienced. As a Christian scholar, I feel the freedom to engage in the construction of theology, offering a new reading of the passion narrative and its significance for Christian faith. I do not, however, have the expertise or the religious positionality to do theology in Judaism and Islam. As such, I do my best to present the scholarship of others within these traditions and to suggest applications of their work that might serve a similar therapeutic function.

First I must clarify a few points. The passion narratives in the Christian scriptures have been used throughout Christian history to justify antisemitism and violence by Christians against Jewish people (Levine 2018; Edwards 2023: 3). But Jesus was a Jewish man executed by Rome, a settler Empire, not by "the Jews." Furthermore, establishing the authorship, motivation, and historicity of the various gospels is the source of deep scholarly debate (and far beyond my expertise to comment on). It is, therefore, difficult to say exactly what, if any, role Judas, the Sanhidrin, or Caiaphas played in Jesus's arrest and ultimate execution by the state. Even if Jesus was betrayed by a Jewish friend and handed over to Rome by the Sanhidrin, as the Gospel narratives describe (See Edwards 2023 for an account of potential anti-Semitic motivations of the gospel writers), such actions cannot be attributed to the Jewish community as a whole any more than any case of religious abuse described in this Element should be attributed to the entire religious tradition in which it took place.

It may nonetheless be notable for Christian survivors of religious trauma that whether one considers Jesus experience as depicted in the canonical gospels or an alternative where Jesus's execution is solely the result of State violence against a perceived threat, Jesus's suffering and death satisfy the characteristics of religious trauma as I have described it throughout this volume. First, according to the canonical story, Jesus and his teaching are contentious within the Jewish community, leading not only to many embracing his spiritual and political message but also to others rejecting it and resenting his ministry to the point of wishing his death (Luke 4, Matthew 12, Mark 2–3, Luke 6, John 10, Mark 14, etc.). He is betrayed by one of his closest friends, and throughout his trial and execution, he is abandoned by the followers with whom he shared a deep spiritual connection. That is, the Bible portrays Jesus as experiencing spiritual and religious betrayal and abuse when (some) religious power aligns itself with state power. If, on the other hand, Jesus was executed by Rome as a perceived Jewish threat to Roman authority without any involvement from his own community, he is nonetheless likely targeted for this abuse not only because of his ethnicity, but also for his revolutionary, and deeply religious and spiritual teachings. Put differently, Jesus is described in Christian scriptures as having experienced religious abuse in the primary sense that I explore in this Element (inflicted by someone or something connected to one's own religious tradition), but could alternatively be understood to have experience it in the secondary sense of a persecution experience (inflicted because of one's religious affiliation) that I acknowledge in Section 2 as a possible source of religious trauma.

Second, after his arrest, Jesus is beaten, mocked, sexually humiliated, possibly sexually assaulted, and ultimately killed via the slow, painful torture of Roman crucifixion. The claim that Jesus was sexually humiliated and possibly assaulted may shock some readers. However, there is historical support for reading the repeated stripping of Jesus's clothing when he is mocked and beaten prior to a (likely) nude crucifixion (the soldiers cast lots for his clothing, including his undergarments) as a form of public sexual humiliation. Crucifixion was a form of state terror, intended not only to punish and humiliate the condemned, but to serve as a warning to others, and forced exposure was a common method of displaying dominance and forced submission in the ancient world. Furthermore, historically, Roman crucifixion often involved sexual violence and genital mutilation. Although we have no direct evidence that Jesus was sexually assaulted in addition to being sexually abused by forced exposure, it is a live historical possibility (Tombs 1999; Tombs 2023).

All these forms of abuse may well have occasioned the neurobiological processes that lead to post-traumatic distress. As Preston Hill argues in dialogue with Rambo, Jesus had a human body that would have "kept the score" of his trauma (Hill 2022), satisfying the 2nd characteristic of religious trauma. Third, and most poignantly, during the crucifixion, Jesus cries out, "my God, my God, why have you forsaken me?!" There is significant theological debate over the metaphysical import of these words. But according to one way of reading this vignette, there is a moment on the cross when the human nature and person of Jesus has an experience as of abandonment by God. On this read, it may well have been that the experience of spiritual, physical, and sexual abuse occasions a disruption in Jesus's own sense of relationship with the Divine. While Hill and Sartor follow Stump in presenting the cry of dereliction as a moment when Jesus only empathizes with the stains on the soul caused by trauma, one could alternatively read it as something stronger than mere empathy: a real, first-personal experience as of alienation from God occasioned by religious trauma. Although merely a possibility rather than something that we can affirm as certainly a part of the experience of the incarnate God, this would satisfying the third characteristic of religious trauma.

Finally, even after the resurrection, Jesus bears the residual effects of trauma in the form of physical wounds. Indeed, these marks become a central witness to Jesus's identity in the Gospel of John. Sometimes referred to as "scars," the Biblical narrative is actually rather vague about the nature of the marks left on Jesus's hands, feet, and side. The Greek word Thomas uses can refer to a mark, an imprint, or a scar. But Jesus invites him to put his hand into his side. This might suggest an open, gaping wound, rather than a fully healed scar, and Shelly Rambo notes that "the Johannine gospel does not tell us whether they are open or closed, exposed or sutured" (Rambo 2017: 18). Regardless of the precise stage of healing, Jesus is unashamed that the marks in his flesh testify to the lasting impact of his suffering (it remains and returns like all trauma) and to his identity (his trauma is a central part of how his followers recognize him).

While it must be done with care and caution, I believe that Christians can simultaneously acknowledge the historical and moral ambiguity of this aspect of their tradition, while still find it significant that the tradition has not considered spiritual abuse, in either the primary or secondary senses, something to which their savior would necessarily be immune. Theologian David Tombs writes, with respect to seeing Jesus as victim of sexual violence, that these claims

> offer insights into a fuller Christian understanding of a God who is in real
> solidarity with the powerless and suffers the worst evils of the world. An
> a priori judgment that Jesus did not and could not suffer sexual abuse may
> accompany an unexamined assumption that Jesus was not in fact fully
> human, a form of the docetic heresy which denies the real form of Jesus'

physical suffering. Refusal to accept that Jesus could have been sexually abused suggests a refusal to accept Christ's full incarnation into human history. To say that Jesus could not have been vulnerable to the worst abuses of human power is to deny that he was truly human at all. (1999: 109)

The same could be said for religious trauma. We do not know the degree to which the passion was religious traumatic for Jesus. But to assume *a priori* that Jesus *could not* have experienced the impact of religious trauma may be to deny Jesus's full humanity.

On Ekstrom's proposal, people who endure religious trauma and a sense of alienation from God in its aftermath may be having a religious experience. They may be having an experience of the same kind as a divine person has had. While I deny that the experience is inherently good because it is "Christ-like," or that it provides a God-justifying reason for allowing the trauma to occur, it seems plausible that some who remain or become Christians in the wake of religious trauma may find it therapeutic to identify with Jesus in this way. That God knows or could know intimately what it is like to experience the pain of religious trauma may make that pain easier to bear. Furthermore, the cry of dereliction could counteract any guilt and shame that accompany the sense of alienation from God. Both Christian communities and survivors themselves tend to think that the spiritual impact of religious trauma is the result of moral or spiritual failure. If only they responded correctly, trusted God more, forgave, or tried harder, they would not feel alienated from God or God's people in the wake of the abuse. Perhaps Jesus's words give the lie to this perspective. Jesus, according to tradition, is sinless and perfect. His sense of abandonment by God cannot be the result of any spiritual failure. The church dare not tell Jesus to buck up, get over it, or move on – that if he just fixed his theology, he would feel God's loving presence. If Jesus could experience alienation without fault, Christians should be slower to blame those who have similar experiences.

Some theological positions maintain that Jesus's experience at this moment in salvation history is utterly unique – that the trinity is broken and that Jesus is literally abandoned by God as he becomes the object of God's wrath – something that no genuine believer will ever experience. On this view, Jesus's experience on the cross could not be understood as resulting from religious abuse, and could not provide grounds for the claim that one can feel abandoned by God without any wrongdoing, guilt, or lack of faith on one's own part (on this view Jesus is abandoned precisely because he bears human guilt). While I think this view is both morally and metaphysically mistaken, even if it were correct, literal abandonment by God and literally bearing the punishment for human sin could itself be a spiritually traumatic experience for Jesus. Even if Jesus really was abandoned by God and no other Christian will ever experience similar abandonment, the fact remains that it seems to some victims of religious trauma that they are being abandoned in the same way, and this may be enough to find some source of comfort in the knowledge that Jesus experienced the same, and worse.

Finally, thinking of religious trauma as the same kind of experience had by a divine person may be instructive for churches who have survivors of religious trauma in their midst. Traditional Christian theology teaches that Jesus freely chose to take on human flesh, "to live and die as one of us," and to accept the spiritual abuse and religious trauma that came with it. Likewise, deep engagement with the experiences of religious trauma survivors and activism on their behalf may itself subject some Christians to actual or vicarious spiritual trauma. If unconflicted faith and a sense of closeness with God unmarred by symptoms of post-traumatic distress are the height of the Christian life, then deep empathetic engagement with those experiencing religious trauma may be too risky. It puts everything at stake. But if the heart of the Christian faith is being like Jesus, then perhaps the risk of caring for survivors and of bearing witness to their experiences is justified, while still remaining a deep, existential and spiritual risk. Genuinely entering into it may hurt us deeply. It may well shake our faith to its core. We, unlike Jesus, may not be able to predict whether our faith will weather such a storm. But perhaps being willing to endure this pain with those impacted by it is how we may come and die like our Lord.

For Jewish survivors there may be a different sense in which religious trauma is the same kind of experience as one had by a divine person. In *The Female Face of God in Auschwitz*, Melissa Raphael suggests such an approach to the suffering of women in the camps (2003). Raphael draws on the Jewish Feminist theological tradition of interpreting Shekinah – God's glory manifest – as a feminine face of God-she, who cares for Israel as she wanders in the wilderness. She suggests that the care women gave to each other in the face of death is where God was in Auschwitz. Acts of care in the face of death are acts of the same kind as those performed by the divine person. If it was difficult to perceive the face of God in Auschwitz, Raphael argues, it was because the personhood of God's people, who manifest God to the world, was itself obscured by dehumanization. "The face of Shekhinah was hidden only in so far as the Jewish faces that imaged her were de-faced by their profanation; burned and dispersed as ash" (55). Raphael is careful to distinguish her picture of God as present and suffering with her people in the camps from the Christian image of the suffering God, because in Judaism God suffers with, but not vicariously for, her people. The suffering of the people and of God is not necessary to fulfill any spiritual or moral debt. It is simply the care of a lover for the beloved.

I do not wish to suggest that suffering religious trauma, just as such, is morally on par with the suffering of the Shoah. However, insofar as it was genocide of a people for whom spirituality is bound up with ethnic identity, it is inconceivable that the trauma of the Shoah did not have explicit spiritual and religious dimensions, as Raphael and her interlocutors make clear. As such, they may be read as grappling with a certain kind of religious trauma. With great care and humility, survivors of other forms of religious trauma within Judaism may find guidance in Raphael's work for grappling with the reality of religious trauma. Perhaps the love and care Jewish survivors and their allies offer one another, affirming humanity and dignity in the face of abuse, is the face of God-she in religious trauma, because it is the same kind of experience/action as one that the divine person has.

Sanctifying suffering when pointing to anything positively meaningful in it, particularly within traditions that present Jesus as a model for others to follow, is always a danger. When embracing (vicarious) suffering as Christ-like, and being Christ-like is an expression of holiness, it is easy to draw the conclusion that one ought to embrace rather than flee abuse. Delores Williams argues that such thinking has often played a role in the way women of color have repeatedly been placed, either by force or by cultural expectation, in surrogacy roles where they bear the weight of the sufferings, labor, and struggles of wealthy white people in their own bodies. For Williams, traditional interpretations of redemptive suffering offer meaning and hope in the face of suffering at the cost of sanctifying oppression, and at the cost of telling those who have already sacrificed the most to keep on sacrificing. It is one thing to tell the privileged that sacrifice is Godly; they already have more than they need in terms of the integrity of the self and material resources. But to tell this to those already suffering the most is to preclude their liberation. She argues that, as an alternative, the Black religious experience should be read through the lens of Hagar's wilderness experience. Hagar is an enslaved woman, forced into surrogacy, driven out of her home into the wilderness. There she encounters God as a God who sees (Williams 1993:141–148). For Williams, a wilderness experience is "a symbolic term used to represent a near-destruction situation in which God gives personal direction to the believer and thereby helps her to make a way out of what she thought was no way" (Williams 1993: 108). Interpreting the Black religious experience as one primarily of God making "a way where there is no way," she calls this the "survival-quality of life tradition" in contrast to the tradition of liberation. God does not liberate Hagar. In fact, for the sake of her survival, he initially sends her back to her oppressors, and she is eventually sent away by them. For her there is no liberation, only survival.

Raphael's account largely escapes Williams's critique. Raphael denies that redemption comes through suffering. God-she is not present in Auschwitz in order to redeem them or anyone else through her suffering. She is present there because her people are present there. Further, Raphael insists that suffering and abjection are not the preconditions for spiritual or ethical virtue, to be sanctified and praised for their own sake. They are simply the sites where community manifests in the camps, given conditions beyond the community's own control. However, while Williams emphasizes survival and quality of life (while also acknowledging that entire generations of enslaved people do not survive), Raphael talks about care and presence even in death. She tells of an "almost iconic nameless old woman with 'hair white as snow' who is remembered for holding in her arms a motherless 1-year-old child as she stood at the edge of the communal pit, about to be shot with the rest of her village by Nazi troops. The old woman sang to the child and tickled him under the chin until he laughed with joy. Then they were shot" (Raphael 2003: 58). Neither offer hope for liberation after trauma. Instead, they suggest finding ways of seeing God even in the face of death.

Williams's reflections on Hagar also suggest a framework for an Islamic therapeutic theodicy. Although Hājar (Hagar) is not mentioned in the Qur'an, her story plays an important role in Muslim tradition. During *hajj* (religious pilgrimage), pilgrims to Mecca commemorate and ritually reenact Hājar's running back and forth between Safa and Marwa in search of water. According to Islamic tradition, when Ibrahīm takes Hājar and Isma'il and abandons them in the desert, Hājar repeatedly asks him why he is doing this, but he remains silent. Finally, Hājar asks if God has told him to abandon them here, and he responds affirmatively. Hājar then declares that God will not allow them to perish. In conversation with Williams, Muslim feminist scholars amina wadud and Jerusha Lamptey argue that in a "Hājar Paradigm" (Wadud 2008; Lamptey 2018) Hajar's life and faith offer a critique and expansion of traditional Islamic theological anthropology. Lamptey points out that Hājar's position as "the foremother of the Islamic tradition ... does not erase the abuse, abandonment, and struggle she faced and endured" (184). Hājar herself was an enslaved person required by people of God to bear the child of her master's husband, abandoned in the desert in the name of God, and left to provide for her family alone, all of which allows us to see her as a survivor of religious abuse and trauma. Lamptey gestures at this possibility when she notes critically that "any intimation that her situation of abandonment and suffering was problematic can be taken as an assault on the broader narrative of origins" (186). Even if, on the traditional account, Hājar trusts God absolutely and has her active partnership with God rewarded by a miraculous spring of water, hers is faith in the midst of struggle and abuse in which God is implicated. Lamptey asserts that her "faithful and deep reliance [did not] remove her fear, pain, struggle, and even anger" (186). If this way of receiving Hājar's story is plausible, then at the heart of Islam, a central spiritual practice honors the actions of a vulnerable, abused woman who experiences religious trauma and yet became the fore-mother of the faithful. This may be a source of comfort to religious trauma survivors like Aisha who struggle to trust God after being mistreated by spiritual leaders in their communities. Perhaps, then, we can expand Ekstrom's account of religious experiences to include experiences like those of divine agents and other religious figures and role models such as prophets and holy women.

5.4 Concluding Thoughts

There is still much unknown, philosophically and psychologically speaking, about religious trauma. But what we do know is that it is common and that it should no longer be ignored. It is difficult to make progress without first understanding the nature of such experiences. That is what this volume aims to offer. But moving forward, the question of post-traumatic spiritual flourishing is one of pressing importance. Countless survivors have come forward. Many communities are, slowly and much too late, taking steps to acknowledge past wrongs and to prevent future harm. But for many, the harm has already been done. Philosophical and psychological investigation into the sorts of community structures and practices that enhance and repair spiritual agency, that foster flourishing in the midst of religiously significant post-traumatic distress, and which include and center the needs of survivors are all necessary if religious communities and philosophy of religion wish to respond appropriately to past wrongs.

References

Adams, M. M. (2013). Praying Angry and Surviving Abuse. *Reverberations: New Directions in the Study of Prayer*, http://forums.ssrc.org/ndsp/author/marilyn-adams/.

Alcoff, L. M. (2007). Epistemologies of Ignorance: Three Types. In S. S. N. Tuana, ed., *Race and Epistemologies of Ignorance*. Albany: State University of New York Press.

Allen, J. G., Fultz, J., Huntoon, J., and Brethour, J. R., Jr. (2002). Pathological Dissociative Taxon Membership, Absorption, and Reported Childhood Trauma in Women with Trauma-Related Disorders. *Journal of Trauma & Dissociation*, **3**(1), 89–110.

Alston, W. P. (2014). *Perceiving God: The Epistemology of Religious Experience*. Ithaca: Cornell University Press.

Anonymous (2021). kashf, spiritual experiences, and corruption: Lessons and reflections from my tariqa experience – In Shaykh's Clothing. September 23. https://inshaykhsclothing.com/kashf-spiritual-experiences-and-corruption-lessons-and-reflections-from-my-tariqa-experience/ (Accessed: August 12, 2023).

Association, A. P. (2013). *Diagnostic and Statistical Manual of Mental Disorders (DSM-5)*. Washington, DC: Booksmith.

Ataria, Y. (2016). Traumatic and Mystical Experiences: The Dark Nights of the Soul. *Journal of Humanistic Psychology*, **56**(4), 331–356.

Barnes, H. A., Hurley, R. A., and Taber, K. H. (2019). Moral Injury and PTSD: Often Co-occurring Yet Mechanistically Different. *The Journal of Neuropsychiatry and Clinical Neurosciences*, **31**(2), A4–103.

Bergmann, M. (2011). Skeptical Theism and The Problem of Evil. In Thomas P. Flint and Michael C. Rea, eds., *The Oxford Handbook of Philosophical Theology*. Oxford: Oxford University Press.

Berkovits, E. (1973). *Faith after the Holocaust*. Jerusalem: KTAV.

Blumenthal, D. R. (1993). *Facing the Abusing God: A Theology of Protest*. Louisville, KY: Westminster John Knox Press.

Bohache, T. (2008). *Christology from the Margins*. Louisville, KY: SCM Press.

Bottoms, B. L., Shaver, P. R., Goodman, G. S., and Qin, J. (1995). In the Name of God: A Profile of Religion-Related Child Abuse. *Journal of Social Issues*, **51**(2), 85–111.

Bottoms, B. L., Nielsen, M., Murray, R., and Filipas, H. (2004). Religion-Related Child Physical Abuse: Characteristics and Psychological Outcomes. *Journal of Aggression, Maltreatment & Trauma*, **8**(1–2), 87–114.

Brison, S. J. (2002). *Aftermath: Violence and the Remaking of a Self*. Princeton: Princeton University Press.

Brown, C. and Augusta-Scott, T. (2007). *Narrative Therapy: Making Meaning, Making Lives*. Thousand Oaks, CA: Sage.

Burley, M. (2020). *A Radical Pluralist Philosophy of Religion: Cross-Cultural, Multireligious, Interdisciplinary*. London: Bloomsbury.

Carter, R. T. (2007). Clarification and Purpose of the Race-Based Traumatic Stress Injury Model. *The Counseling Psychologist*, **35**(1), 144–154.

Caruth, C. (1996). *Unclaimed Experience: Trauma, Narrative, and History*. Baltimore, MD: John Hopkins University Press.

Castillo, R. (1994). Spirit Possession in South Asia, Dissociation or Hysteria. *Culture, Medicine and Psychiatry*, **18**, 1–21.

Chapin, B. (2003). *Hierarchy, envy and spirit possession: Case studies of internalization among Sinhala women in central Sri Lanka*. Ph.D. Dissertation, San Diego: University of California.

Clare, E. (2014). Meditations on Natural Worlds, Disabled Bodies, and a Politics of Cure. In S. Iovino and S. Oppermann, eds., *Material Ecocriticism*. Indiana University Press, pp. 204–218.

Cockayne, J. (2019). Smelling God: Olfaction as Religious Experience. In B. Hereth and K. Timpe, eds., *The Lost Sheep in Philosophy of Religion*. New York: Routledge, pp. 97–119.

Cone, J. H. (2011). *The Cross and the Lynching Tree*. Maryknoll: Orbis Books.

Courtois, C. A. and Ford, J. D. (2015). *Treatment of Complex Trauma: A Sequenced, Relationship-Based Approach*. New York: Guilford.

Crosby, A. (2021). *Surviving Religious Violence: A Study on Religious Harm and Trauma in Contemporary US American Christianity*. Master's Thesis. Duke Divinity School.

De Cruz, H. (2020). Believing to Belong: Addressing the Novice-Expert Problem in Polarized Scientific Communication. *Social Epistemology*, **34**(5), 440–452.

Dehan, N. and Levi, Z. (2009). Spiritual Abuse: An Additional Dimension of Abuse Experienced by Abused Haredi (Ultraorthodox) Jewish Wives. *Violence against Women*, **15**(11), 1294–1310.

der Kolk, B. (2015). *The Body Keeps the Score: Brain, Mind, and Body in the Healing of Trauma*. New York: Penguin Publishing Group.

Dotson, K. (2012). A Cautionary Tale: On Limiting Epistemic Oppression. *Frontiers: A Journal of Women Studies*, **33**(1), 24–47.

Doyle, T. P. (2009). The Spiritual Trauma Experienced by Victims of Sexual Abuse by Catholic Clergy. *Pastoral Psychology*, **58**(3), 239–260.

Edwards, J. C. (2023). *Crucified: The Christian Invention of the Jewish Executioners of Jesus*. Minneapolis, MN: Fortress Press.

Ekstrom, L. W. (2014). A Christian Theodicy. In J. P. McBrayer and D. Howard-Snyder, eds., *The Blackwell Companion to the Problem of Evil*. Oxford, UK: John Wiley & Sons, pp. 266–280.

Ekstrom, L. W. (2021). *God, Suffering, and the Value of Free Will*. New York: Oxford University Press.

Fassin, Didier and Rechtman, Richard. (2009). *The Empire of Trauma : An Inquiry into the Condition of Victimhood*. Princeton, NJ: Princeton University Press.

Feldman, D. (2012). *Unorthodox: The Scandalous Rejection of My Hasidic Roots*. New York: Simon and Schuster.

Felitti, V. J., Anda, R. F., Nordenberg, D., *et al.* (1998). Relationship of Childhood Abuse and Household Dysfunction to Many of the Leading Causes of Death in Adults. *American Journal of Preventive Medicine*, **14**(4), 245–258.

Foody, K. and Tarm, M. (2023). *Hundreds of Catholic Clergy in Illinois Sexually Abused Thousands of Children, AG Finds, PBS NewsHour*. www.pbs.org/newshour/nation/hundreds-of-catholic-clergy-in-illinois-sexually-abused-thousands-of-children-ag-finds (Accessed: August 12, 2023).

Fricker, M. (2007). *Epistemic Injustice: Power and the Ethics of Knowing*. Oxford: Oxford University Press.

Gerber, M. M., Boals, A., and Schuettler, D. (2011). The Unique Contributions of Positive and Negative Religious Coping to Posttraumatic Growth and PTSD. *Psychology of Religion and Spirituality*, **3**(4), 298–307.

Goldsmith, R. E., Martin, C. G., and Smith, C. P. (2014). Systemic Trauma. *Journal of Trauma & Dissociation*, **15**(2), 117–132.

Gonda, X., Dome, P., Erdelyi-Hamza, B., *et al.* (2022). Invisible Wounds: Suturing the Gap between the Neurobiology, Conventional and Emerging Therapies for Posttraumatic Stress Disorder. *European Neuropsychopharmacology*, **61**, 17–29.

Griffin, B. J., Purcell, N., Burkman, K., *et al.* (2019). Moral Injury: An Integrative Review. *Journal of Traumatic Stress*, **32**(3), 350–362.

Griffioen, A. (2016). Religious Experience without Belief? Toward an Imaginative Account of Religious Engagement. In T. Hardtke, U. Schmiedel, and T. Tan, eds., *Religious Experience Revisited: Expressing the Inexpressible?* Boston, MA: Brill, pp. 73–88.

(2018). Therapeutic Theodicy? Suffering, Struggle, and the Shift from the God's-Eye View. *Religions*, **9**(4), 99.

(2021). *Religious Experience*. New York: Cambridge University Press.

Hacking, Ian (1995). *Rewriting The Soul: Multiple Personality and the Sciences of Memory*. Princeton: Princetone University Press.

Harper, L. (2013a). *Silent No Longer: Lani Harper's Story, Part Two | Homeschoolers Anonymous, Homeschoolers Anonymous*. https://home schoolersanonymous.wordpress.com/2013/11/07/silent-no-longer-lani-harpers-story-part-two/ (Accessed: June 29, 2023).

(2013b). *Silent No Longer: Lani Harper's Story, Part One | Homeschoolers Anonymous, Homeschoolers Anonymous*. https://homeschoolersanon ymous.wordpress.com/2013/11/05/silent-no-longer-lani-harpers-story-part-one/ (Accessed: June 29, 2023).

Harris, M. J. (2016). "But Now My Eye Has Seen You": Yissurin Shel Ahavah as Divine Intimacy Theodicy. *The Torah U-Madda Journal*, **17**, 64–92.

Harris, N. B. (2018). *The Deepest Well: Healing the Long-Term Effects of Childhood Adversity*. Boston, MA: Houghton Mifflin Harcourt.

Hereth, B. (2022). Mary, Did You Consent? *Religious Studies*, **58**(4), 677–700.

Herman, J. L. (2015). *Trauma and Recovery: The Aftermath of Violence – From Domestic Abuse to Political Terror*. New York: Basic Books.

Hill, P. (2022). Christ's Body Keeps the Score: Trauma-Informed Theology and the Neuroscience of PTSD. *TheoLogica: An International Journal for Philosophy of Religion and Philosophical Theology*, **7**(1), 102–120.

Hill, P. and Sartor, D. (2022). Attachment Theory and the Cry of Dereliction. *TheoLogica: An International Journal for Philosophy of Religion and Philosophical Theology*, **6**(1), 150–177.

Hochman, S. (1992). *Sinead's Defense: She Says She Seeks Truth, Los Angeles Times*. www.latimes.com/archives/la-xpm-1992-10-24-ca-655-story.html (Accessed: March 20, 2024).

Hollier, J., Clifton, S., and Smith-Merry, J. (2022). Mechanisms of Religious Trauma amongst Queer People in Australia's Evangelical Churches. *Clinical Social Work Journal*, **50**, 275–285.

Holmes, S. C., Facemire, V. C., and DaFonseca, A. M. (2016). Expanding Criterion a for Posttraumatic Stress Disorder: Considering the Deleterious Impact of Oppression. *Traumatology*, **22**(4), 314–321.

van Inwagen, P. (2006). *The Problem of Evil: The Gifford Lectures Delivered in the University of St. Andrews in 2003*. New York: Oxford University Press.

Issa, M. G. (2021). *We Need to Talk about Spiritual Abuse in Our Community, Muslim Girl*. https://muslimgirl.com/we-need-to-talk-about-spiritual-abuse-in-our-community/ (Accessed: August 3, 2023).

Jackson, F. (1986). What Mary Didn't Know. *Journal of Philosophy*, **83**(5), 291–295.

James, W. (1902). *The Varieties of Religious Experience: A Study in Human Nature*. New York: The Modern library.

Jones, T. W., Power, J., and Jones, T. M. (2022). Religious Trauma and Moral Injury from LGBTQA+ Conversion Practices. *Social Science & Medicine*, **305**, 1–9.

Kennedy, P. and Drebing, C. E. (2002). Abuse and Religious Experience: A Study of Religiously Committed Evangelical Adults. *Mental Health, Religion & Culture*, **5**(3), 225–237.

Koch, D. and Edstrom, L. (2022). Development of the Spiritual Harm and Abuse Scale. *Journal for the Scientific Study of Religion*, **61**(2), 476–506.

Kroll, J., Fiszdon, J., and Crosby, R. D. (1996). Childhood Abuse and Three Measures of Altered States of Consciousness (Dissociation, Absorption and Mysticism) in a Female Outpatient Sample. *Journal of Personality Disorders*, **10**(4), 345–354.

Lamptey, J. T. (2018). *Divine Words, Female Voices: Muslima Explorations in Comparative Feminist Theology*. Oxford University Press.

Levine, A.-J. (2018). Christian Privilege, Christian Fragility, and the Gospel of John. In A. Reinhartz, ed., *The Gospel of John and Jewish-Christian Relations*. Lanham: Lexington/Fortress.

Lifshitz, M., Van Elk, M., and Luhrmann, T. M. (2019). Absorption and Spiritual Experience: A Review of Evidence and Potential Mechanisms. *Consciousness and Cognition*, **73**, 1–15.

Lindemann, H. (2001). *Damaged Identities, Narrative Repair*. Ithaca: Cornell University Press.

Litz, B. T., Stein, N., Delaney, E., *et al.* (2009). Moral Injury and Moral Repair in War Veterans: A Preliminary Model and Intervention Strategy. *Clinical Psychology Review*, **29**(8), 695–706.

Luhrmann, T. M. (2004). Yearning for God: Trance as a Culturally Specific Practice and Its Implications for Understanding Dissociative Disorders. *Journal of Trauma & Dissociation*, **5**(2), 101–129.

Luhrmann, T. M. (Tanya, M.) (2005). The Art of Hearing God: Absorption, Dissociation, and Contemporary American Spirituality. *Spiritus: A Journal of Christian Spirituality*, **5**(2), 133–157.

McAdams, D. (2008). Personal Narratives and the Life Story. In O. John, R. Robins, and L. A. Pervine, eds., *Handbook of Personality: Theory and Research*. New York: Guilford Press, pp. 242–262.

McLaughlin, B. R. (1994). Devastated Spirituality: The Impact of Clergy Sexual Abuse on the Survivor's Relationship with God and the Church. *Sexual Addiction & Compulsivity*, **1**(2), 145–158.

Medina, J. (2012). *The Epistemology of Resistance: Gender and Racial Oppression, Epistemic Injustice, and Resistant Imaginations*. Oxford: Oxford University.

Mills, C. W. (1997). *The Racial Contract*. Ithaca, NY: Cornell University Press.

Moltmann, J. (1993). *The Crucified God: The Cross of Christ as the Foundation and Criticism of Christian Theology*. London. SCM Press.

Morrigan, C. (2021). *Trauma Magic*. Self-published.

Narayan, U. (2004). The Project of Feminist Epistemology: Perspectives from a Non-Western Feminist. In S. Harding, ed., *Feminist Standpoint Theory Reader: Intellectual and Political Controversies*. New York: Routledge, pp. 213–2024.

Nobakht, H. N. and Dale, K. Y. (2018). An Exploration of the Roles of Trauma and Dissociation in Mystical Experiences and Near-Death Experiences. *Journal of Spirituality in Mental Health*, **20**(4), 321–332.

Nobakht, H. N. and Yngvar Dale, K. (2018). The Importance of Religious/Ritual Abuse as a Traumatic Predictor of Dissociation. *Journal of Interpersonal Violence*, **33**(23), 3575–3588.

Office of the Illinois Attorney General (2023). *Report on Catholic Clergy Child Sex Abuse in Illinois*. Office of the Illinois Attorney General. https:// clergyreport.illinoisattorneygeneral.gov/download/report.pdf (Accessed: January 14, 2024).

Ortega, M. (2006). Being Lovingly, Knowingly Ignorant: White Feminism and Women of Color. *Hypatia*, **21**(3), 56–74.

Panchuk, M. (2018). The Shattered Spiritual Self: A Philosophical Exploration of Religious Trauma. *Res Philosophica*, **95**(3), 505–530.

(2020). Distorting Concepts, Obscured Experiences: Hermeneutical Injustice in Religious Trauma and Spiritual Violence. *Hypatia*, **35**(4), 607–625.

(2021). Has God Indeed Said? Skeptical Theism and Scriptural Hermeneutics. *Journal of Analytic Theology*, **9**, 45–66.

(2023). What Doesn't Kill Me Makes Me Stronger? Post-Traumatic Growth and the Problem of Suffering. *Religious Studies*, First View, 1–17.

Pargament, K. I., Magyar, G. M., Benore, E., and Mahoney, A. (2005). Sacrilege: A Study of Sacred Loss and Desecration and Their Implications for Health and Well-Being in a Community Sample. *Journal for the Scientific Study of Religion* **44**(1), 59–78.

Parra, A. (2019). Negative Experiences in Childhood, Parental Style, and Resilience among People Reporting Paranormal Experiences. *Journal of Nervous & Mental Disease*, **207**(4), 264–270.

Pasquale, T. (2015). *Sacred Wounds: A Path to Healing from Spiritual Trauma*. St. Louis, MO: Chalice Press.

Paul, L. A. (2014). *Transformative Experience*. Oxford: Oxford University Press.

Piepzna-Samarasinha, L. L. (2018). *Care Work: Dreaming Disability Justice.* Vancouver: Arsenal Pulp Press.

Plantinga, A. (1989). *God, Freedom, and Evil.* Grand Rapids, MI: Wm. B. Eerdmans.

(2000). *Warranted Christian Belief.* Oxford: Oxford University Press.

Pohlhaus, G. (2012). Relational Knowing and Epistemic Injustice: Toward a Theory of Willful Hermeneutical Ignorance. *Hypatia*, **27**(4), 715–735.

(2020). Gaslighting and Echoing, or Why Collective Epistemic Resistance Is Not a "Witch Hunt." *Hypatia*, **35**(4), 674–686.

Pollan, M. (2019). *How to Change Your Mind: What the New Science of Psychedelics Teaches Us about Consciousness, Dying, Addiction, Depression, and Transcendence.* New York: Penguin.

Prusak, J. and Schab, A. (2022). Spiritual Trauma as a Manifestation of Religious and Spiritual Struggles in Female Victims of Sexual Abuse in Adolescence or Young Adulthood in the Catholic Church in Poland. *Archive for the Psychology of Religion*, **44**(1), 40–65.

Qasim, D. (2019). Fallout: A Real Account of Calling Out an Abusive Shaykh – In Shaykh's Clothing. December 17. https://inshaykhsclothing.com/accounts-of-spiritual-abuse/fallout-a-real-account-of-calling-out-an-abusive-shaykh/ (Accessed: August 12, 2023).

Rambo, S. (2010). *Spirit and Trauma: A Theology of Remaining.* Louisville, KY: Westminster John Knox Press.

(2017). *Resurrecting Wounds: Living in the Afterlife of Trauma.* Waco, TX: Baylor University Press.

Raphael, M. (2003). *The Female Face of God in Auschwitz: A Jewish Feminist Theology of the Holocaust.* New York: Routledge.

(2004). The Price of (Masculine) Freedom and Becoming: A Feminist Response to Eliezer Berkovits's Post-Holocaust Free Will Defence of God's Non-intervention in Auschwitz. In P. S. Anderson and B. Clack, eds., *Feminist Philosophy of Religion: Critical Perspectives.* New York: Routledge, pp. 136–150.

Rea, M. (2013). Skeptical theism and the "too much skepticism" objection. In P. J. McBrayer and D. Howard-Snyder, eds., *The Blackwell Companion to the Problem of Evil.* Oxford, UK: Wiley, pp. 482–506.

Rea, M. (2022). The Metaphysics of the Narrative Self. *Journal of the American Philosophical Association*, **8**(4), 586–603.

Rea, M. C. (2018). *The Hiddenness of God.* Oxford: Oxford University Press.

Ricœur, P. (1992). *Oneself as Another.* Chicago: University of Chicago Press.

Root, M. (1992). Impact of Trauma on Personality. In L.S. Brown and M. Ballou, eds., *Personality and Psychopathology: Feminist Reappraisals*. New York: Guilford Press Publications, pp. 229–265.

Rossetti, S. J. (1995). The Impact of Child Sexual Abuse on Attitudes toward God and the Catholic Church. *Child Abuse & Neglect*, **19**(12), 1469–1481.

Rouzati, N. (2018). Evil and Human Suffering in Islamic Thought – Towards a Mystical Theodicy. *Religions*, **9**(2), 47.

Saraiya, T. and Lopez-Castro, T. (2016). Ashamed and Afraid: A Scoping Review of the Role of Shame in Post-Traumatic Stress Disorder (PTSD). *Journal of Clinical Medicine*, **5**(11), 94.

Singh, N. (2023). Open Letter Concerning Clergy Abuse. Episcopal Accountability. https://episcopalaccountability.com/open_letters/nivedhan_singh (Accessed: July 20, 2023).

Smith, S. (2004). Exploring the Interaction of Trauma and Spirituality. *Traumatology*, **10**(4), 231–243.

Stump, E. (2010). *Wandering in Darkness: Narrative and the Problem of Suffering*. Oxford: Oxford University Press.

Suryani, L. K. and Jensen, G. D. (1993). *Trance and Possession in Bali: A Window on Western Multiple Personality Disorder and Suicide*. Kuala Lumpur: Oxford.

Swinburne, R. (2004). *The Existence of God*. Oxford: Clarendon Press.

Szymanski, D. M. and Balsam, K. F. (2011). Insidious Trauma: Examining the Relationship between Heterosexism and Lesbians' PTSD Symptoms. *Traumatology*, **17**(2), 4–13.

Timpe, K. (2019). Moral Ecology, Disabilities, and Human Agency. *Res Philosophica*, **96**(1), 17–41.

Tobin, T. (2016). Spiritual Violence, Gender, and Sexuality: Implications for Seeking and Dwelling among Some Catholic Women and LGBT Catholics. In P. Rossi, ed., *Spiritual Violence, Gender, and Sexuality: Seekers and Dwellers: Plurality and Wholeness in a Time of Secularity*. Washington, DC: The Council for Research in Values and Philosophy, pp. 133–166.

Tobin, T. W. and Moon, D. (2020). Sacramental Shame in Black Churches: How Racism and Respectability Politics Shape the Experiences of Black LGBTQ and Same-Gender-Loving Christians. In M. Panchuk and M. Rea, eds., *Voices from the Edge: Centring Marginalized Perspectives in Analytic Theology*. Oxford: Oxford University Press, pp. 141–165.

Tombs, D. (1999). Crucifixion, State Terror, and Sexual Abuse. *Union Seminary Quarterly Review*, **53**, 89–109.

    (2022). *The Crucifixion of Jesus: Torture, Sexual Abuse, and the Scandal of the Cross*. London: Routledge.

Truth and Reconciliation Commission (2015). *The Survivors Speak: A Report of the Truth and Reconciliation Commission of Canada.* Winnipeg: Truth and Reconciliation Commission of Canada.

Van Dyke, C. (2018). What Has History to Do with Philosophy? Insights from the Medieval Contemplative Tradition. *Proceedings of the British Academy*, **214**, 155–170.

Waley, M. I. *et al.* (2022). *Spiritual Abuse in the Sufi Order Headed by Shaykh Nuh Keller.* https://muslimmatters.org/2022/06/06/spiritual-abuse-sufi-nuh-keller/ (Accessed: August 3, 2023).

Wadud, A. (2008). *Inside the Gender Jihad: Women's Reform in Islam.* New York: Simon and Schuster.

Ward, D. J. (2011). The Lived Experience of Spiritual Abuse. *Mental Health, Religion & Culture*, **14**(9), 899–915.

Watson, G. (1987). Responsibility and the Limits of Evil: Variations on a Strawsonian Theme. In F. Schoeman, ed., *Responsibility, Character, and the Emotions*. New York: Cambridge University Press, pp. 256–286.

Watson, L. B., DeBlaere, C., Langrehr, K. J., Zelaya, D. G., Flores, M. J. (2016). The Influence of Multiple Oppressions on Women of Color's Experiences with Insidious Trauma. *Journal of Counseling Psychology*, **63**(6), 656–667.

Wiesel, E. (2006). *Night.* Translated by M. Wiesel. New York: Hill and Want.

Williams, D. S. (1993). *Sisters in the Wilderness: The Challenge of Womanist God-Talk.* Orbis Books.

Winell, M. (2011) Religious Trauma Syndrome (Series of 3 articles). *Cognitive Behavioural Therapy Today*, **39**(2), 16–18.

World Health Organization (no date). *International Classification of Diseases 11th Revision the Global Standard for Diagnostic Health Information.* World Health Organization.

Zalcberg, S. (2017). The Place of Culture and Religion in Patterns of Disclosure and Reporting Sexual Abuse of Males: A Case Study of Ultra Orthodox Male Victims. *Journal of Child Sexual Abuse*, **26**(5), 590–607.

Acknowledgments

This Element owes its existence to countless survivors of religious trauma who have shared their stories and wisdom with me. I could not have researched this difficult topic without the support of my husband Yuriy Panchuk, daughter Miroslava Panchuk, and my dear friends Grey Sun, Marie Thearose, Blake Hereth, Jon Parsons, Kevin Timpe, and Kristin Irwin. I also owe a special debt of gratitude to Grey Sun, Kevin Timpe, Michael Rea, Samuel Lebens, Stephen Rayburn, and Amy-Jill Levine for helpful feedback on various portions.

Cambridge Elements ⹀

The Problems of God

Series Editor
Michael L. Peterson
Asbury Theological Seminary

Michael L. Peterson is Professor of Philosophy at Asbury Theological Seminary.
He is the author of *God and Evil* (Routledge); *Monotheism, Suffering, and Evil*
(Cambridge University Press); *With All Your Mind* (University of Notre Dame Press);
C. S. Lewis and the Christian Worldview (Oxford University Press); *Evil and the Christian God*
(Baker Book House); and *Philosophy of Education: Issues and Options* (Intervarsity Press).
He is co-author of *Reason and Religious Belief* (Oxford University Press); *Science,
Evolution, and Religion: A Debate about Atheism and Theism* (Oxford University Press); and
Biology, Religion, and Philosophy (Cambridge University Press). He is editor of
The Problem of Evil: Selected Readings (University of Notre Dame Press). He is co-editor of
Philosophy of Religion: Selected Readings (Oxford University Press) and *Contemporary
Debates in Philosophy of Religion* (Wiley-Blackwell). He served as General Editor of the
Blackwell monograph series Exploring Philosophy of Religion and is founding Managing
Editor of the journal *Faith and Philosophy*.

About the Series
This series explores problems related to God, such as the human quest for God
or gods, contemplation of God, and critique and rejection of God. Concise,
authoritative volumes in this series will reflect the methods of a variety of disciplines,
including philosophy of religion, theology, religious studies, and sociology.

Cambridge Elements ⸗

The Problems of God

Elements in the Series

God and Value Judgments
Kevin Kinghorn

God and the Problem of Evidential Ambiguity
Max Baker-Hytch

The Problem of Animal Pain
Victoria Campbell

God and Astrobiology
Richard Playford, Stephen Bullivant and Janet Siefert

God, Religious Extremism and Violence
Matthew Rowley

C.S. Lewis and the Problem of God
David Werther

Embodiment, Dependence, and God
Kevin Timpe

God and Happiness
Matthew Shea

The Problem of Divine Personality
Andrew M. Bailey and Bradley Rettler

The Trinity
Scott M. Williams

God and the Problem of Epistemic Defeaters
Joshua Thurow

Religious Trauma
Michelle Panchuk

A full series listing is available at: www.cambridge.org/EPOG